THIRD EDITION

INTRO

Skills for Success
READING AND WRITING

Jennifer Bixby | Joe McVeigh

OXFORD
UNIVERSITY PRESS

OXFORD
UNIVERSITY PRESS

198 Madison Avenue
New York, NY 10016 USA

Great Clarendon Street, Oxford, OX2 6DP, United Kingdom

Oxford University Press is a department of the University of Oxford.
It furthers the University's objective of excellence in research, scholarship,
and education by publishing worldwide. Oxford is a registered trade
mark of Oxford University Press in the UK and in certain other countries

ISBN: 978 0 19 490391 2   Student Book Intro with iQ Online pack
ISBN: 978 0 19 490367 7   Student Book Intro as pack component
ISBN: 978 0 19 490427 8   iQ Online student website

Printed in China

This book is printed on paper from certified and well-managed sources

ACKNOWLEDGMENTS

Back cover photograph: Oxford University Press building/David Fisher

Illustrations by: Mark Duffin p.76; 5W Infographics p.78, p.91; Karen Minot
p.98; Greg Paprocki p.86.

*The Publishers would like to thank the following for their kind permission to reproduce
photographs and other copyright material*: 123rf: pp.4 (woman laughing/asife),
41 (fruit and vegetables/Kurhan), 52 (woman in thought/Ion Chiosea),
63 (tropical beach/vacclav), (give someone a ride/Mark Bowden), 82 (puzzled
student/Antonio Guillem), 111 (woman jogging/ferli); Alamy: pp.6 (Rob/
SeventyFour Images), 8 (helpful/DGLimages), 15 (Jacob/Antonio Guillem
Fernández), 27 (German classroom/Kuttig – People), 28 (tall and small/
Radius Images), 29 (tennis training/Cavan Images), 34 (Japanese classroom/
Payless Images, Inc.), 38 (women at Lakshmi Puja festival/robertharding),
40 (Japanese wedding/David Warren), 41 (Gilroy Garlic Fesitival/Mariusz
Jurgielewicz), 42 (cheese rolling/robertharding), (herring stall/Mikhail
Olykaynen), 61 (family camping/Hero Images Inc.), 65 (friends having
dinner party/DGLimages), 66 (hand painting bowl/Jake Lyell), 72 (modern
architecture in Seattle/Stefano Politi Markovina), 80 (Middlebury/Jon
Arnold Images Ltd), 84 (NEMO Science Center/Ulrich Doering), 93 (Kansas
City Public Library/Nancy Hoyt Belcher), 115 (woman preparing healthy
food/Ammentorp Photography), 116 (multiethnic community/Andrew
Fox), 126 (red bicycle path/dpa picture alliance), 139 (merry go round/
Carol Bond), 143 (blind man listening to audio/Disability Images),
150 (Cambridge graduates/Jeremy Pembrey), 160 (woman checking mail/
Tetra Images), 163 (medical robot/Ekkasit Keatsirikul); Getty: pp.cover
(rice fields/AlexGcS/RooM), 2 (viewing art in gallery/Robert Alexander),
4 (man looking at clothes/Indeed), 6 (Carlos/pidjoe), 9 (Cristiano Ronaldo/
Simon Stacpoole/Offside), 17 (Lauren/Inti St Clair), 19 (mosaic of portrait
photos/Plume Creative), 20 (students in auditorium/Klaus Vedfelt),
23 (boat school/Jonas Gratzer), 40 (barbecue/Andersen Ross Photography
Inc), 46 (Chinese steamboat meal/Jordan Lye), 55 (children eating
toffee apples/BLOOMimage), 56 (people riding a rollercoaster/Chad
Slattery), 60 (couple sightseeing/Hinterhaus Productions), 61 (tourists
in Antarctica/Martin Harvey), 71 (men having barbecue/Caiaimage/Tom
Merton), 94 (woman eating burger at computer/Matthias Heitmann),
102 (woman drinking coffee/John Fedele), 103 (Biggest Loser contestant/
NBC), (woman playing video game/Micko1986), 118 (brownstone building/
Blend Images – Peter Dressel), 120 (female friends socialising/Nastasic),
(woman looking out of window/recep-bg), 128 (students in discussion/
asiseeit), 129 (Mongolian landscape with gers/Tuul & Bruno Morandi),
131 (glass fronted library/Westend61), 138 (reading a transport map/
Rosanna U), 144 (Hans Wiberg/Tristan Fewings / Stringer), 147 (blind
person surfing/NICOLAS TUCAT), 149 (Hayat Sindi/Jonathan Torgovnik),
156 (teenager taking driving test/monkeybusinessimages), 162 (metal joint/
Jan-Otto); Oxford University Press: pp.4 (overweight man/Monkey Business
Images), 120 (Vancouver/Shutterstock/Dan Breckwoldt), 130 (pollution/
Shutterstock/M. Shcherbyna), 134 (Dubai/Shutterstock/mohamed
alwerdany); Shutterstock: pp.6 (Kate/Monkey Business Images), 8 (serious/
Tatiana Frank), 14 (diverse group of people/Rawpixel.com), 22 (flooding/
Sk Hasan Ali), 24 (rock climbing/Alexander Rochau), 27 (Kenyan classroom/
Billy Miaron), 30 (student planting project/Syda Productions), 36 (students
studying in library/wavebreakmedia), 37 (schoolgirl in museum/Monkey
Business Images), 40 (strawberry sundae/kostrez), (ripe tomatoes/Skanaks),
41 (garlic/OShuma), (herring/HETIZIA), 42 (white truffles/Fabrizio Esposito),
48 (pizza in brick oven/risteski goce), 49 (chicken noodle soup/paulzhuk),
59 (empty pockets/jajam_e), 64 (highlighting/A.J. Pictures), 74 (cutlery
drawer/brizmaker), 76 (exterior of dorms/f11photo), 96 (man eating salad/
ZephyrMedia), 100 (soda/NaughtyNut), 105 (making smoothie/Impact
Photography), 107 (cyclist/GP Studio), 112 (student working late/Sam
Wordley), 125 (Humboldt University/Massimo Todaro), 126 (outdoor winter
market/franz12), 133 (city skyline/Joshua Haviv), 136 (public underground/
joyfull), 149 (scientist in lab/Matej Kastelic); Third Party: pp.81 (exterior
of Self-Reliance House/Middlebury College Solar Decathlon Team 2011),
(interior of Self-Reliance House/Middlebury College Solar Decathlon Team
2011), 140 (Aldo Amenta graduating/FIU/Aldo Amenta), 144 (Be My Eyes
user/Be My Eyes).

We would like to acknowledge the teachers from all over the world who participated in the development process and review of *Q: Skills for Success* Third Edition.

USA

Kate Austin, Avila University, MO; **Sydney Bassett**, Auburn Global University, AL; **Michael Beamer**, USC, CA; **Renae Betten**, CBU, CA; **Pepper Boyer**, Auburn Global University, AL; **Marina Broeder**, Mission College, CA; **Thomas Brynmore**, Auburn Global University, AL; **Britta Burton**, Mission College, CA; **Kathleen Castello**, Mission College, CA; **Teresa Cheung**, North Shore Community College, MA; **Shantall Colebrooke**, Auburn Global University, AL; **Kyle Cooper**, Troy University, AL; **Elizabeth Cox**, Auburn Global University, AL; **Ashley Ekers**, Auburn Global University, AL; **Rhonda Farley**, Los Rios Community College, CA; **Marcus Frame**, Troy University, AL; **Lora Glaser**, Mission College, CA; **Hala Hamka**, Henry Ford College, MI; **Shelley A. Harrington**, Henry Ford College, MI; **Barrett J. Heusch**, Troy University, AL; **Beth Hill**, St. Charles Community College, MO; **Patty Jones**, Troy University, AL; **Tom Justice**, North Shore Community College, MA; **Robert Klein**, Troy University, AL; **Patrick Maestas**, Auburn Global University, AL; **Elizabeth Merchant**, Auburn Global University, AL; **Rosemary Miketa**, Henry Ford College, MI; **Myo Myint**, Mission College, CA; **Lance Noe**, Troy University, AL; **Irene Pannatier**, Auburn Global University, AL; **Annie Percy**, Troy University, AL; **Erin Robinson**, Troy University, AL; **Juliane Rosner**, Mission College, CA; **Mary Stevens**, North Shore Community College, MA; **Pamela Stewart**, Henry Ford College, MI; **Karen Tucker**, Georgia Tech, GA; **Loreley Wheeler**, North Shore Community College, MA; **Amanda Wilcox**, Auburn Global University, AL; **Heike Williams**, Auburn Global University, AL

Canada

Angelika Brunel, Collège Ahuntsic, QC; **David Butler**, English Language Institute, BC; **Paul Edwards**, Kwantlen Polytechnic University, BC; **Cody Hawver**, University of British Columbia, BC; **Olivera Jovovic**, Kwantlen Polytechnic University, BC; **Tami Moffatt**, University of British Columbia, BC; **Dana Pynn**, Vancouver Island University, BC

Latin America

Georgette Barreda, SENATI, Peru; **Claudia Cecilia Díaz Romero**, Colegio América, Mexico; **Jeferson Ferro**, Uninter, Brazil; **Mayda Hernández**, English Center, Mexico; **Jose Ixtaccihusatl**, Instituto Tecnológico de Tecomatlán, Mexico; **Andreas Paulus Pabst**, CBA Idiomas, Brazil; **Amanda Carla Pas**, Instituição de Ensino Santa Izildinha, Brazil; **Allen Quesada Pacheco**, University of Costa Rica, Costa Rica; **Rolando Sánchez**, Escuela Normal de Tecámac, Mexico; **Luis Vasquez**, CESNO, Mexico

Asia

Asami Atsuko, Jissen Women's University, Japan; **Rene Bouchard**, Chinzei Keiai Gakuen, Japan; **Francis Brannen**, Sangmyung University, South Korea; **Haeyun Cho**, Sogang University, South Korea; **Daniel Craig**, Sangmyung University, South Korea; **Thomas Cuming**, Royal Melbourne Institute of Technology, Vietnam; **Nguyen Duc Dat**, OISP, Vietnam; **Wayne Devitte**, Tokai University, Japan; **James D. Dunn**, Tokai University, Japan; **Fergus Hann**, Tokai University, Japan; **Michael Hood**, Nihon University College of Commerce, Japan; **Hideyuki Kashimoto**, Shijonawate High School, Japan; **David Kennedy**, Nihon University, Japan; **Anna Youngna Kim**, Sogang University, South Korea; **Jae Phil Kim**, Sogang University, South Korea; **Jaganathan Krishnasamy**, GB Academy, Malaysia; **Peter Laver**, Incheon National University, South Korea; **Hung Hoang Le**, Ho Chi Minh City University of Technology, Vietnam; **Hyon Sook Lee**, Sogang University, South Korea; **Ji-seon Lee**, Iruda English Institute, South Korea; **Joo Young Lee**, Sogang University, South Korea; **Phung Tu Luc**, Ho Chi Minh City University of Technology, Vietnam; **Richard Mansbridge**, Hoa Sen University, Vietnam; **Kahoko Matsumoto**, Tokai University, Japan; **Elizabeth May**, Sangmyung University, South Korea; **Naoyuki Naganuma**, Tokai University, Japan; **Hiroko Nishikage**, Taisho University, Japan;

Yongjun Park, Sangji University, South Korea; **Paul Rogers**, Dongguk University, South Korea; **Scott Schafer**, Inha University, South Korea; **Michael Schvaudner**, Tokai University, Japan; **Brendan Smith**, RMIT University, School of Languages and English, Vietnam; **Peter Snashall**, Huachiew Chalermprakiet University, Thailand; **Makoto Takeda**, Sendai Third Senior High School, Japan; **Peter Talley**, Mahidol University, Faculty of ICT, Thailand; **Byron Thigpen**, Sogang University, South Korea; **Junko Yamaai**, Tokai University, Japan; **Junji Yamada**, Taisho University, Japan; **Sayoko Yamashita**, Jissen Women's University, Japan; **Masami Yukimori**, Taisho University, Japan

Middle East and North Africa

Sajjad Ahmad, Taibah University, Saudi Arabia; **Basma Alansari**, Taibah University, Saudi Arabia; **Marwa Al-ashqar**, Taibah University, Saudi Arabia; **Dr. Rashid Al-Khawaldeh**, Taibah University, Saudi Arabia; **Mohamed Almohamed**, Taibah University, Saudi Arabia; **Dr Musaad Alrahaili**, Taibah University, Saudi Arabia; **Hala Al Sammar**, Kuwait University, Kuwait; **Ahmed Alshammari**, Taibah University, Saudi Arabia; **Ahmed Alshamy**, Taibah University, Saudi Arabia; **Doniazad sultan AlShraideh**, Taibah University, Saudi Arabia; **Sahar Amer**, Taibah University, Saudi Arabia; **Nabeela Azam**, Taibah University, Saudi Arabia; **Hassan Bashir, Edex**, Saudi Arabia; **Rachel Batchilder**, College of the North Atlantic, Qatar; **Nicole Cuddie**, Community College of Qatar, Qatar; **Mahdi Duris**, King Saud University, Saudi Arabia; **Ahmed Ege**, Institute of Public Administration, Saudi Arabia; **Magda Fadle**, Victoria College, Egypt; **Mohammed Hassan**, Taibah University, Saudi Arabia; **Tom Hodgson**, Community College of Qatar, Qatar; **Ayub Agbar Khan**, Taibah University, Saudi Arabia; **Cynthia Le Joncour**, Taibah University, Saudi Arabia; **Ruari Alexander MacLeod**, Community College of Qatar, Qatar; **Nasir Mahmood**, Taibah University, Saudi Arabia; **Duria Salih Mahmoud**, Taibah University, Saudi Arabia; **Ameera McKoy**, Taibah University, Saudi Arabia; **Chaker Mhamdi**, Buraimi University College, Oman; **Baraa Shiekh Mohamed**, Community College of Qatar, Qatar; **Abduleelah Mohammed**, Taibah University, Saudi Arabia; **Shumaila Nasir**, Taibah University, Saudi Arabia; **Kevin Onwordi**, Taibah University, Saudi Arabia; **Dr. Navid Rahmani**, Community College of Qatar, Qatar; **Dr. Sabah Salman Sabbah**, Community College of Qatar, Qatar; **Salih**, Taibah University, Saudi Arabia; **Verna Santos-Nafrada**, King Saud University, Saudi Arabia; **Gamal Abdelfattah Shehata**, Taibah University, Saudi Arabia; **Ron Stefan**, Institute of Public Administration, Saudi Arabia; **Dr. Saad Torki**, Imam Abdulrahman Bin Faisal University, Dammam, Saudi Arabia; **Silvia Yafai**, Applied Technology High School/Secondary Technical School, UAE; **Mahmood Zar**, Taibah University, Saudi Arabia; **Thouraya Zheni**, Taibah University, Saudi Arabia

Turkey

Sema Babacan, Istanbul Medipol University; **Bilge Çöllüoğlu Yakar**, Bilkent University; **Liana Corniel**, Koc University; **Savas Geylanioglu**, Izmir Bahcesehir Science and Technology College; **Öznur Güler**, Giresun University; **Selen Bilginer Halefoğlu**, Maltepe University; **Ahmet Konukoğlu**, Hasan Kalyoncu University; **Mehmet Salih Yoğun**, Gaziantep Hasan Kalyoncu University; **Fatih Yücel**, Beykent University

Europe

Amina Al Hashamia, University of Exeter, UK; **Irina Gerasimova**, Saint-Petersburg Mining University, Russia; **Jodi**, Las Dominicas, Spain; **Marina Khanykova**, School 179, Russia; **Oksana Postnikova**, Lingua Practica, Russia; **Nina Vasilchenko**, Soho-Bridge Language School, Russia

CRITICAL THINKING

The unique critical thinking approach of the *Q: Skills for Success* series has been further enhanced in the Third Edition. New features help you analyze, synthesize, and develop your ideas.

Unit question
The thought-provoking unit questions engage you with the topic and provide a critical thinking framework for the unit.

UNIT QUESTION

What kind of person are you?

A. Discuss these questions with your classmates.

1. Your personality describes what is special about you. What is your personality? Are you a quiet person or a noisy person? Are you funny or serious?

2. What do you look like?

3. Look at the photo. Which faces look happy? Surprised? Funny? Serious? How do you feel most of the time?

B. Listen to *The Q Classroom* online. Then answer these questions.

Analysis
You can discuss your opinion of each reading text and analyze how it changes your perspective on the unit question.

WRITE WHAT YOU THINK

A. DISCUSS Ask and answer these questions with a partner. Look back at your Quick Write on page 41. Think about what you learned.

1. What is your favorite celebration?
2. When do you usually have this celebration?
3. What special foods do you eat? Why?
4. What is your favorite food at this celebration?

B. SYNTHESIZE Think about the reading and the unit video as you discuss these questions. Then choose and write the number of one question. Then write 3–5 sentences.

1. What kind of food is very special to you?
2. How would you describe your favorite celebration?

NEW! Critical Thinking Strategy with video
Each unit includes a Critical Thinking Strategy with activities to give you step-by-step guidance in critical analysis of texts. An accompanying instructional video (available on iQ Online) provides extra support and examples.

NEW! Bloom's Taxonomy
Blue activity headings integrate verbs from Bloom's Taxonomy to help you see how each activity develops critical thinking skills.

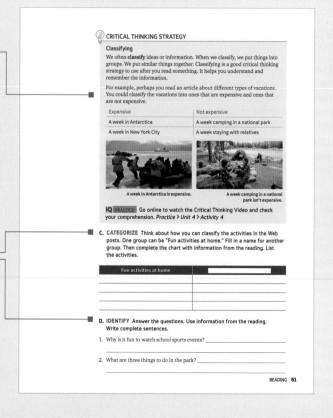

CRITICAL THINKING STRATEGY

Classifying

We often **classify** ideas or information. When we classify, we put things into groups. We put similar things together. Classifying is a good critical thinking strategy to use after you read something. It helps you understand and remember the information.

For example, perhaps you read an article about different types of vacations. You could classify the vacations into ones that are expensive and ones that are not expensive.

Expensive	Not expensive
A week in Antarctica	A week camping in a national park
A week in New York City	A week staying with relatives

A week in Antarctica is expensive.

A week camping in a national park isn't expensive.

iQ PRACTICE Go online to watch the Critical Thinking Video and check your comprehension. *Practice > Unit 4 > Activity 4*

C. CATEGORIZE Think about how you can classify the activities in the Web posts. One group can be "Fun activities at home." Fill in a name for another group. Then complete the chart with information from the reading. List the activities.

Fun activities at home	

D. IDENTIFY Answer the questions. Use information from the reading. Write complete sentences.

1. Why is it fun to watch school sports events? _____

2. What are three things to do in the park? _____

READING **61**

iv

THREE TYPES OF VIDEO

UNIT VIDEO

The unit videos include high-interest documentaries and reports on a wide variety of subjects, all linked to the unit topic and question.

NEW! "Work with the Video" pages guide you in watching, understanding, and discussing the unit videos. The activities help you see the connection to the Unit Question and the other texts in the unit.

CRITICAL THINKING VIDEO

NEW! Narrated by the Q series authors, these short videos give you further instruction into the Critical Thinking Strategy of each unit using engaging images and graphics. You can use them to get a deeper understanding of the Critical Thinking Strategy.

SKILLS VIDEO

NEW! These instructional videos provide illustrated explanations of skills and grammar points in the Student Book. They can be viewed in class or assigned for a flipped classroom, for homework, or for review. One skill video is available for every unit.

Easily access all videos in the Resources section of iQ Online.

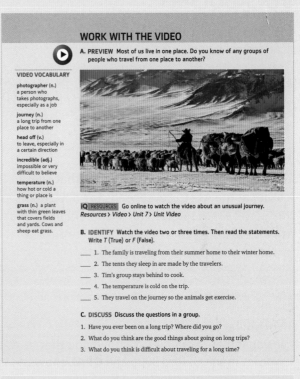

WORK WITH THE VIDEO

A. PREVIEW Most of us live in one place. Do you know of any groups of people who travel from one place to another?

VIDEO VOCABULARY

photographer (n.) a person who takes photographs, especially as a job

journey (n.) a long trip from one place to another

head off (v.) to leave, especially in a certain direction

incredible (adj.) impossible or very difficult to believe

temperature (n.) how hot or cold a thing or place is

grass (n.) a plant with thin green leaves that covers fields and yards. Cows and sheep eat grass.

iQ RESOURCES Go online to watch the video about an unusual journey. Resources > Video > Unit 7 > Unit Video

B. IDENTIFY Watch the video two or three times. Then read the statements. Write T (True) or F (False).

____ 1. The family is traveling from their summer home to their winter home.

____ 2. The tents they sleep in are made by the travelers.

____ 3. Tim's group stays behind to cook.

____ 4. The temperature is cold on the trip.

____ 5. They travel on the journey so the animals get exercise.

C. DISCUSS Discuss the questions in a group.

1. Have you ever been on a long trip? Where did you go?

2. What do you think are the good things about going on long trips?

3. What do you think is difficult about traveling for a long time?

How to compare and contrast

Venn Diagram

Firefighter — Both — Police Officer

fights fires — *help people* — *fights crime*

stays at the station until called — *have dangerous jobs* — *works on the street*

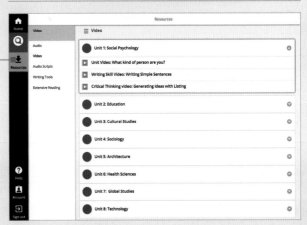

Resources

Video

Unit 1: Social Psychology

Unit Video: What kind of person are you?

Writing Skill Video: Writing Simple Sentences

Critical Thinking video: Generating Ideas with Listing

Unit 2: Education

Unit 3: Cultural Studies

Unit 4: Sociology

Unit 5: Architecture

Unit 6: Health Sciences

Unit 7: Global Studies

Unit 8: Technology

VOCABULARY

A research-based vocabulary program focuses on the words you need to know academically and professionally.

The vocabulary syllabus in *Q: Skills for Success* is correlated to the CEFR (see page 164) and linked to two word lists: the Oxford 3000 and the OPAL (Oxford Phrasal Academic Lexicon).

♀ OXFORD 3000

The Oxford 3000 lists the core words that every learner at the A1–B2 level needs to know. Items in the word list are selected for their frequency and usefulness from the Oxford English Corpus (a database of over 2 billion words).

Vocabulary Key
In vocabulary activities, ♀ shows you the word is in the Oxford 3000 and **OPAL** shows you the word or phrase is in the OPAL.

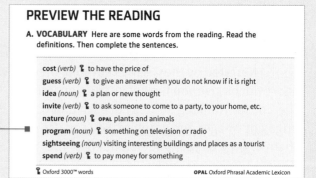

PREVIEW THE READING

A. VOCABULARY Here are some words from the reading. Read the definitions. Then complete the sentences.

cost *(verb)* ♀ to have the price of
guess *(verb)* ♀ to give an answer when you do not know if it is right
idea *(noun)* ♀ a plan or new thought
invite *(verb)* ♀ to ask someone to come to a party, to your home, etc.
nature *(noun)* ♀ **OPAL** plants and animals
program *(noun)* ♀ something on television or radio
sightseeing *(noun)* visiting interesting buildings and places as a tourist
spend *(verb)* ♀ to pay money for something

♀ Oxford 3000™ words   **OPAL** Oxford Phrasal Academic Lexicon

OPAL
OXFORD PHRASAL ACADEMIC LEXICON

NEW! The OPAL is a collection of four word lists that provide an essential guide to the most important words and phrases to know for academic English. The word lists are based on the Oxford Corpus of Academic English and the British Academic Spoken English corpus. The OPAL includes both spoken and written academic English and both individual words and longer phrases.

Academic Language tips in the Student Book give information about how words and phrases from the OPAL are used and offer help with features such as collocations and phrasal verbs.

Santiago Posted: 12 hours ago	Our family likes going to the park. We take walks and enjoy **nature** there. Sometimes we have coffee and watch people. We try to **guess** their names and jobs. Try it!

ACADEMIC LANGUAGE
The phrase *as well as* is common in academic writing. It is used to add a point.

OPAL
Oxford Phrasal Academic Lexicon

Carlos San Salvador Posted: 4 hours ago	Re: How do you have fun without much money? **Invite** some friends to your house and cook together! My friends and I cook together once a month. First, we decide on a meal. Then we shop for the food and prepare the dishes. We usually cook food from a different country. My favorite was from Brazil. It's fun to eat with friends as well as try new recipes.
Khalid Cairo Posted: 2 hours ago	Re: How do you have fun without much money? I like to just stay home and watch TV. There are lots of good **programs**, and it's free. That's the best way to have fun.
Rob London Posted: 2 hours ago	Re: How do you have fun without much money? **Sightseeing** is fun, and you don't have to be a tourist. You can take a vacation in your own city. Walk around and enjoy the famous places.
James New York Posted: 1 hour ago	Re: How do you have fun without much money? Thanks, everyone, for all of your ideas. I'll try some of them!

EXTENSIVE READING

NEW! Extensive Reading is a program of reading for pleasure at a level that matches your language ability.

There are many benefits to Extensive Reading:

- It helps you to become a better reader in general.
- It helps to increase your reading speed.
- It can improve your reading comprehension.
- It increases your vocabulary range.
- It can improve your grammar and writing skills.
- It's great for motivation—reading something that is interesting for its own sake.

Each unit of *Q: Skills for Success* Third Edition has been aligned to an Oxford Graded Reader based on the appropriate topic and level of language proficiency. The first chapter of each recommended graded reader can be downloaded from iQ Online Resources.

UNIT 1

UNIT 2

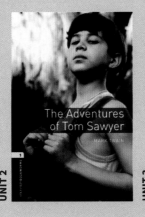

UNIT 3

UNIT 4

UNIT 5

UNIT 6

UNIT 7

UNIT 8

iQ ONLINE extends your learning beyond the classroom.

- Practice activities provide essential skills practice and support.
- Automatic grading and progress reports show you what you have mastered and where you still need more practice.
- Discussion Board to discuss the Unit Questions helps you develop your critical thinking.
- Writing Tutor helps you practice your academic writing skills.
- Essential resources such as audio and video are easy to access anytime.

NEW TO THE THIRD EDITION

- Site is optimized for mobile use so you can use it on your phone.
- An updated interface allows easy navigation around the activities, tests, resources, and scores.
- New Critical Thinking Videos expand on the Critical Thinking Strategies in the Student Book.
- Extensive Reading program helps you improve your vocabulary and reading skills.

How to use
iQ ONLINE

Go to **Practice** to find additional practice and support to complement your learning in the classroom.

Go to **Resources** to find
- All Student Book video
- All Student Book audio
- Critical Thinking videos
- Skills videos
- Extensive Reading

Go to **Messages** and **Discussion Board** to communicate with your teacher and classmates.

Online tests assigned by your teacher help you assess your progress and see where you still need more practice.

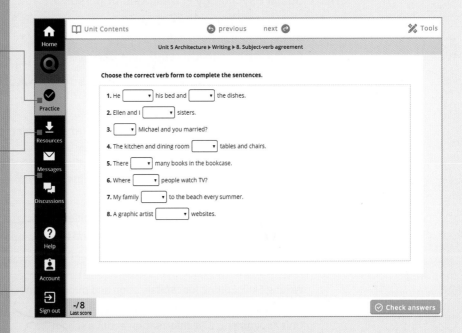

Progress bar shows you how many activities you have completed.

View your scores for all activities.

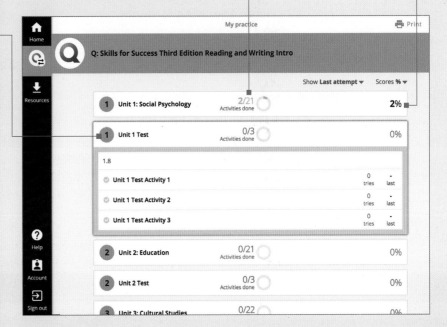

CONTENTS

Social Psychology

VOCABULARY	using descriptive adjectives
READING	identifying topics and main ideas
CRITICAL THINKING	generating ideas with listing
WRITING	writing simple sentences
GRAMMAR	present of *be*; simple present affirmative statements

What kind of person are you?

A. Discuss these questions with your classmates.

1. Your personality describes what is special about you. What is your personality? Are you a quiet person or a noisy person? Are you funny or serious?

2. What do you look like?

3. Look at the photo. Which faces look happy? Surprised? Funny? Serious? How do you feel most of the time?

B. Listen to *The Q Classroom* online. Then answer these questions.

1. Which student is a good student? Which student does not talk a lot? Which student likes to go out? Which student is a serious person?

2. Which student is most like you? Why?

iQ PRACTICE Go to the online discussion board to discuss the Unit Question with your classmates. *Practice > Unit 1 > Activity 1*

UNIT
OBJECTIVE Read the magazine article. Find information and ideas to write about your personality, appearance, and interests.

READING

OBJECTIVE ▶

What Kind of Person Are You?

You are going to read a magazine article about different kinds of people. Use the article to find information and ideas for your Unit Assignment.

PREVIEW THE READING

A. VOCABULARY Here are some words from the reading. Read the sentences. Then circle the meaning of the underlined words.

Toshi likes to buy new clothes.

Maria is very funny.

Paulo is overweight.

1. Toshi likes to buy new <u>clothes</u>.

   a. Toshi likes to buy shirts and pants.

   b. Toshi likes to buy books and magazines.

2. Please <u>describe</u> your brother. Is he tall? What color is his hair?

   a. Help your brother.

   b. Tell me about your brother.

3. Sam is very <u>friendly</u>. He likes to meet new people.

   a. Sam is kind and helpful.

   b. Sam is quiet and shy.

4. Maria is very <u>funny</u>.

   a. Maria makes people laugh.

   b. Maria goes to parties.

5. Paulo exercises. But he's <u>overweight</u>.

   a. Paulo is not strong.

   b. Paulo is not thin.

6. They <u>meet</u> classmates in a new class.

   (a.) They see and talk with classmates for the first time.

   b. They work in an office.

7. Andrew is <u>thin</u>.

   (a.) Andrew is not large.

   b. Andrew has black hair.

8. I don't <u>wear</u> jeans to work.

   a. I don't wash my jeans before work.

   (b.) I don't put on jeans for work.

B. APPLY Complete the sentences with the words from Activity A. (You will not use all the words.)

1. I'm not thin. I'm _overweight_ .

2. Can you _describe_ your father? What does he look like?

3. I like to go shopping. I like to buy _clothes_ .

4. He likes to _wear_ jeans. He says they are comfortable.

5. Mary likes to _meet_ new people.

6. Mary is _friendly_ . She talks to everyone.

iQ PRACTICE Go online for more practice with the vocabulary.
Practice > Unit 1 > Activities 2–3

TIP FOR SUCCESS

Before you read a text, look at the title. Then look at the pictures. What do they tell you about the text?

C. PREVIEW The magazine article describes different kinds of people. Look at the photos in the article on page 6. Write one word to describe each person.

1. Carlos is _quiet and shy_ .

2. Rob is _tall_ .

3. Kate isn't _neat. She is messy._

D. QUICK WRITE Describe yourself. Answer the questions. Use this section for your Unit Assignment.

1. What do you look like? _I feel lost._

2. What do you like to do? _I like to visit all countries._

3. Describe your personality. _I'm quiet sometime._

"social

WORK WITH THE READING

 A. INVESTIGATE Read the magazine article. Find information about different kinds of people.

WHAT KIND OF PERSON ARE YOU?

This week *Talk Magazine* is asking readers questions. Read each question and the two answers. Which answer **describes** you? Check (✓) one answer for each question.

1. Are you a **friendly** person?

☐ Yes, I am. I have a lot of friends, and I like to **meet** new people. *(James, 18)*

☑ I'm a nice guy, but I'm quiet. I have two or three good friends. I talk to them a lot. But with other people, I'm shy. *(Carlos, 23)*

2. Are you interested in fashion?

☑ I usually **wear** jeans and T-shirts. I don't care about people's **clothes**. I'm more interested in someone's personality. *(Hassan, 22)*

☐ I like to dress well. I'm interested in fashion. *(Matt, 21)*

Carlos

3. How tall are you?

☐ I'm 6 feet 3 inches (192 centimeters) tall. I play basketball for City University. *(Rob, 20)*

☑ I'm only about 5 feet 9 inches (179 centimeters). But my two brothers are both very tall—about 6 feet 5 inches (198 centimeters)! All three of us are **thin**. We aren't **overweight**. *(David, 19)*

4. Are you a neat person?

☑ I don't have time to clean. I go to school, and I also have a part-time job. I'm always busy! *(Kate, 21)*

☑ I'm very busy, but I clean my room every day. I'm a very neat person. *(Amanda, 18)*

Rob

5. Are you a **funny** person?

☑ I study a lot, but I also like to have fun. But I don't think I'm funny. *(Sarah, 21)*

☐ I love to laugh and tell funny stories. *(Emma, 24)*

6. What is your best subject in school?

☐ I'm good at math. It's my favorite subject. For some people, math is hard. For me, it is easy. *(Khalid, 18)*

☑ My best subjects are English and French. I also speak Spanish! *(Pablo, 17)*

Kate

B. CATEGORIZE Read the statements. Write *T* (true) or *F* (false). Then correct each false statement to make it true.

_T_ 1. James likes to meet new people.
_F_ 2. Carlos is not very shy.
_F_ 3. Hassan is interested in clothes.
_F_ 4. David is tall.
_F_ 5. Kate is a very neat person.

_T_ 6. Amanda's room is neat.
_T_ 7. Sarah studies very hard.
_T_ 8. Emma is a funny person.
_F_ 9. Math is not easy for Khalid.
_T_ 10. Pablo is good at English.

C. IDENTIFY Match the person's name with the description.

_b_ 1. Hassan
_e_ 2. Kate
_h_ 3. Khalid
_c_ 4. Rob
_a_ 5. Carlos
_i_ 6. Pablo
_g_ 7. Emma
_d_ 8. David
_f_ 9. Sarah

a. is shy with other people
b. doesn't care about clothes
c. plays basketball
d. is thin
e. doesn't have time to clean
f. studies a lot
g. likes to tell funny stories
h. likes math
i. speaks French and Spanish

D. APPLY Complete the statements. Use the words from the box.

| busy | funny | neat | speaks | subject |
| friendly | interested | personality | studies | thin |

1. Amanda is a(n) _neat_ person.
2. James is very _friendly_.
3. Math is not a difficult _subject_ for Khalid.
4. Pablo _speaks_ Spanish.
5. Matt is _interested_ in fashion.
6. Hassan is interested in a person's _personality_.
7. Sarah _studies_ a lot.
8. David and his brothers are all _thin_.
9. Emma is _funny_.
10. Kate is always _busy_.

iQ PRACTICE Go online for additional reading and comprehension.
Practice › Unit 1 › Activity 4

We use **descriptive adjectives** to describe people.

Adjectives for appearance	Adjectives for personality
Height: tall, short, average height **Weight:** overweight, thin, average weight **Hair color:** blond, brown, red, black, gray	kind, friendly, helpful, nice shy, quiet smart, intelligent funny, serious

Serious

Helpful

A. APPLY Circle the correct words to complete the statements.

1. He's *tall / (thin) / kind* because he doesn't eat a lot.
2. Talal reads a lot of books. He is very *(intelligent) / blond / helpful*.
3. I laughed because he is a *nice / friendly / (funny) guy*.
4. Aldo doesn't talk much. He is *short / helpful / (shy)*.
5. Sultan is a good basketball player because he is *thin / (tall) / blond*.
6. Aicha studies very hard. She is *helpful / (serious) / thin*.
7. This class is easy for her. She is *funny / (smart) / shy*.
8. Thank you very much. You are very *(helpful) / quiet / overweight*.

B. APPLY Match the words with their opposites.

__c__ 1. friendly   a. neat

__d__ 2. tall   b. serious

__b__ 3. funny   c. shy

__e__ 4. overweight   d. short

__a__ 5. messy   e. thin

C. COMPOSE What other words describe people? Write them in the chart. Then write five sentences (on the next page) using the words.

Words to describe appearance	Words to describe personality

1. _____

2. _____

3. _____

4. _____

5. _____

iQ PRACTICE Go online for more practice with using descriptive adjectives. *Practice > Unit 1 > Activity 5*

READING SKILL Identifying topics and main ideas

Every paragraph has a **topic** and a **main idea**.

- You can usually say the topic in one or two words. To identify the topic, ask this question: *What is this paragraph about?*

  In this paragraph, the topic is *my brother*. The topic repeats in the paragraph.

  > My brother, Miteb, is very popular. Everyone likes him. Why? For one thing, he is very friendly. He laughs a lot, and he tells funny and interesting stories. He makes people happy. For these reasons, my brother has a lot of friends.

TIP FOR SUCCESS

The main idea is often in the first or last sentence of a paragraph, but not always.

- You can usually say the main idea in a short sentence. To identify the main idea, ask this question: *What is the most important idea in this paragraph?*

  In the paragraph above, the main idea is *My brother, Miteb, is very popular.* The other sentences in the paragraph explain this idea.

INVESTIGATE Read the article. Then answer the questions on page 10.

Cristiano Ronaldo

1   Cristiano Ronaldo is a famous soccer player. He is from Portugal. He plays for a soccer team in Italy. The team is called *Juventus*.

2   Ronaldo is good at soccer. In his free time, he is also interested in business. He owns two clothing stores in Portugal. One store is in Lisbon, and one is in Madeira.

3   Each year, his team pays him $30 million. Companies also pay him to wear their clothes and shoes. Cristiano Ronaldo is an extremely rich man.

4   Ronaldo is also very generous. He uses his money to help people around the world. Sometimes he gives his money to people after a flood or an earthquake. He is a nice guy!

1. What is the topic of the reading? _Christiano rornado_

2. What is the main idea of paragraph 1?

   (a.) Ronaldo is a famous soccer player.   b. His team is called Juventus.

3. What is the main idea of paragraph 2?

   a. One store is in Lisbon.   (b.) Ronaldo is interested in business.

4. What is the main idea of paragraph 3?

   a. Companies pay Ronaldo to wear their clothes.   (b.) Ronaldo is a rich man.

5. What is the main idea of paragraph 4?

   a. Ronaldo is a serious person.   (b.) He gives his money to people.

iQ PRACTICE Go online for more practice with identifying topics and main ideas.
Practice > Unit 1 > Activity 6

WORK WITH THE VIDEO

A. PREVIEW Do you look like someone in your family? Do you have a similar personality to someone in your family? Describe them.

VIDEO VOCABULARY

twins (n.) two people who have the same mother and were born at the same time

boss (n.) a person who is in charge of other people at work

talkative (adj.) liking to talk a lot

outgoing (adj.) friendly and interested in other people and new experiences

comfortable (adj.) nice to be in or to wear

iQ RESOURCES Go online to watch the video about twins.
Resources > Video > Unit 1 > Unit Video

B. CATEGORIZE Watch the video two or three times. Complete the diagram with the words from the box.

average height	interested in animals	quiet and serious
friendly	love games	red hair
helpful	outgoing	wants to be a games designer

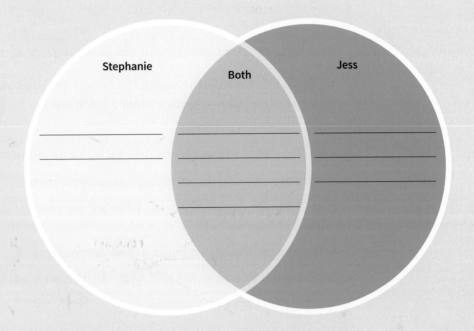

Stephanie

Both

Jess

C. DISCUSS Discuss the questions in a group.

1. Do you know twins (or brothers and sisters) who are very similar? How are they similar? How are they different?

2. Do you know an outgoing person? What does the person like to do?

3. We usually enjoy spending time with people who are similar to us. Do you have a friend or classmate who is different from you? What can you learn from that person?

Generating ideas with listing

When you **generate ideas**, you think of ideas before you write. One way to generate ideas is to make a **list**. For example, to describe a friend, you can make a list of descriptive words:

Description		Personality	
short	brown hair	smart	quiet
thin	brown eyes	funny	helpful

After you generate ideas with a list, it is easy to write sentences.

iQ PRACTICE Go online to watch the Critical Thinking Video and check your comprehension. *Practice > Unit 1 > Activity 7*

D. DISCUSS Work with a partner. Use listing to generate ideas.

1. List three words that describe both you and your partner.

2. Ask, "What are you interested in? What are you good at?" List your partner's answers.

3. Write sentences using the information from your lists.

   My partner is interested in _____.   My partner is good at _____.

4. Compare sentences with your partner.

E. SYNTHESIZE Think about the reading and the unit video as you read these questions. List words to generate ideas.

1. Who is your best friend? What does he or she look like?

   _____

2. Describe your friend's personality. _____

3. What is your friend interested in? _____

 # WRITE WHAT YOU THINK

CREATE Write 3–4 sentences to describe your friend. Use ideas from Activity B.

_____

_____

_____

_____

WRITING

OBJECTIVE ▶

At the end of this unit, you are going to write about your personality, appearance, and interests. Your sentences will include information from the reading, the unit video, and your own ideas.

WRITING SKILL Writing simple sentences

A **simple sentence** in English needs a **subject** and a **verb**. The subject performs the action. Usually the subject comes at the beginning of the sentence. The subject is a noun or a pronoun.

> **Tom** goes to school.
> **Dana** likes basketball.
> **She** is good at math.

A sentence can have more than one subject. Use the word *and* with two subjects.

> Ahmed **and** Salim are from Oman.   John **and** Mary enjoy sports.

The verb is a word that says what someone does or what happens.

> Asako **eats** lunch every day.
> Cristiano Ronaldo **plays** soccer.
> The students **relax** on their vacation.

iQ RESOURCES Go online to watch the Writing Skill Video.
Resources > Video > Unit 1 > Writing Skill Video

WRITING TIP

When you write, be sure that every sentence has a subject and a verb.

A. IDENTIFY Underline the subjects. Circle the verbs.

1. David (is) tall.

2. (I) usually (wear) jeans and T-shirts.

3. Sarah (studies) very hard.

4. Steve (is) very funny.

5. Nat (likes) soccer.

6. Liz enjoys new clothes.

B. APPLY Put the words in the correct order to make simple sentences.

1. likes / television / Pablo _Pablo likes tv._

2. English / studies / Maria _Maria likes/studies English._

3. many books / Fatima / reads _Fatima reads many book._

4. cleans / her room / Emma _Emma clean her room._

5. very friendly / are / Ken and Hiroki _K and H are very friendly_

iQ PRACTICE Go online for more practice with simple sentences.
Practice > Unit 1 > Activity 8

adverb

Use the **present form of the verb *be*** to identify and describe people and things.

Affirmative and negative statements

subject	*be*	*(not)*	
I	**am**		a student.
You / We / They	**are**	**(not)**	tall.
He / She / It	**is**		from Portugal.

- A contraction makes two words into one word. It has an apostrophe (').

  I am = I'm   He is = He's
  You are = You're   She is = She's
  They are = They're It is = It's

- There are two negative contractions for *are not*.

  're not   aren't
  They**'re not** short.   You **aren't** tall.

- There are two negative contractions for *is not*.

  's not   isn't
  She**'s not** American.   He **isn't** from England.

To ask information questions, begin with a *wh-* word + *be*.

Asking information questions				Answers
wh- word	*be*	subject		
Who	**is**	Fahad's friend?		Sam **is** Fahad's friend.
What	**are**	his interests?		His interests **are** soccer and travel.
Where	**are**	you	from?	I **am** from Saudi Arabia.

Jacob

A. APPLY Complete the paragraph with *am*, *is*, or *are*.

My name _____is_____ Jacob. I __am__ (2) from Canada. I _____am_____ (3) tall and my hair _____is_____ (4) very short. Right now, I _____am_____ (5) a student in Mexico. I _____am_____ (6) interested in science. My school _____is_____ (7) for international students. The students _____are_____ (8) from all over the world. I __am__ (9) shy, but it _____is_____ (10) easy to make friends at my school. My classmates _____are_____ (11) very friendly. Sometimes they _____are_____ (12) serious, too.

B. APPLY Complete the sentences. Use the correct affirmative or negative form of *be*. Use contractions.

1. John _____isn't_____ overweight. He weighs only 120 pounds (54 kilos).
2. You talk a lot. You _____aren't_____ quiet.
3. I'm not Canadian. I _____'m_____ from Kuwait.
4. I _____'m not_____ shy. I like to meet new people.
5. They _____aren't_____ good at basketball because they're very short.
6. She _____She isn't_____ a student. She's a teacher.

TIP FOR SUCCESS
A question ends with a question mark (?).

C. APPLY Put the words in the correct order to make questions. Then answer the questions.

1. who / teacher / your / is ___Who is your teacher?___
   ___my teacher is kathy / kathy is my teacher.___
2. interests / what / your / are ___What are your interests.___
   ___I'm interests in math and mechanics.___
3. you / are / what / at / good ___what are you good at?___
   ___I'm good at soccer___
4. are / you / where / from ___where are you from?___
   ___I'm from Africa.___
5. your / when / is / exam ___when is your exam?___
   ___my axam is on wednesday.___

The **simple present** describes habits, facts, or feelings.

| Rasha **eats** breakfast every morning. | Sarah **feels** happy today. |
| Matt **goes** to Brown University. | Rob **likes** to cook. |

Affirmative statements

subject	verb	
I / You / We / They	**come**	from Australia.
He / She / It	**comes**	

Use the base verb + -s or -es after *he*, *she*, and *it*.

Add -*s* after most verbs.	get**s**, like**s**, listen**s**, play**s**
Add -*es* after -*ch*, -*sh*, or -*o*.	do**es**, go**es**, wash**es**, watch**es**
If the verb ends in a consonant + -*y*, change the *y* to *i* and add -*es*.	cr**ies**, fl**ies**, stud**ies**, tr**ies**
Some verbs have an irregular third-person form.	have → has

D. APPLY Complete the sentences. Use the correct form of the verbs from the box.

go	have	read	study	take	wash	watch

1. They _watch_ TV every night at 8:00.
2. Matt _goes_ to school every day.
3. Rob _washes_ his car every weekend. It's a very clean car!
4. Claire _reads_ the newspaper every day.
5. We _take_ a trip every summer.
6. I _have_ brown hair.
7. He _studies_ in the library in the afternoon.

iQ PRACTICE Go online for more practice with the present of *be* and simple present affirmative statements. *Practice > Unit 1 > Activity 9*

iQ PRACTICE Go online for the Grammar Expansion: Simple present with habits, facts, and feelings. *Practice > Unit 1 > Activity 10*

UNIT ASSIGNMENT

OBJECTIVE ▶

Write sentences to describe yourself

In this assignment, you are going to write about your personality, appearance, and interests. Think about the Unit Question, "What kind of person are you?" Use the reading, the unit video, and your work in this unit. Look at the Self-Assessment checklist on page 18.

iQ PRACTICE Go online to the Writing Tutor to read a writing model.
Practice > Unit 1 > Activity 11

A. BRAINSTORM Read the information about Lauren. Rewrite each sentence. Make it true for you. Change the words or use *not*.

I am from China. I am not from England.

Home

Lauren Baker

My appearance and background

I am from England.
I am 20 years old.
My hair is blond.
I'm about average height.

My personality

I am very friendly.
I like new people.

My interests

I enjoy reading and school.
I like clothes and fashion.
I am interested in science and history.
I am good at sports and English.

B. **WRITE** Use your brainstorm sentences to answer these questions about yourself. Write two sentences for each question.

1. a. What do you look like?

    b. What are you like? Describe your personality.

    c. What are you interested in?

    d. What are you good at?

2. Use descriptive adjectives to add more information.

iQ RESOURCES   Go online to download and complete the outline for the answers to the questions. *Resources > Writing Tools > Unit 1 > Outline*

iQ PRACTICE   Go online to the Writing Tutor to write your assignment. *Practice > Unit 1 > Activity 12*

iQ RESOURCES   Go online to download the peer review worksheet. *Resources > Writing Tools > Unit 1 > Peer Review Worksheet*

C. **REVISE** Review your sentences with a partner. Read your partner's sentences. Then use the peer review worksheet. Discuss the review with your partner.

D. **EDIT AND REWRITE** Complete the Self-Assessment checklist. Make final changes to your sentences. Be prepared to hand in your work or discuss it in class.

SELF-ASSESSMENT	Yes	No
Do you use descriptive adjectives?	☐	☐
Does every sentence have a subject and a verb?	☐	☐
Do you use the present of *be* correctly?	☐	☐
Do you use contractions correctly?	☐	☐
Do you use the simple present correctly in affirmative statements?	☐	☐
Do you use vocabulary from the unit?	☐	☐

E. **REFLECT** Discuss these questions with a partner or group.

1. What is something new you learned in this unit?

2. Look back at the Unit Question—What kind of person are you? Is your answer different now than when you started the unit? If yes, how is it different?

iQ PRACTICE   Go to the online discussion board to discuss the questions. *Practice > Unit 1 > Activity 13*

TRACK YOUR SUCCESS

iQ PRACTICE Go online to check the words and phrases you have learned in this unit. *Practice > Unit 1 > Activity 14*

Check (✓) the skills you learned. If you need more work on a skill, refer to the page(s) in parentheses.

VOCABULARY	☐ I can use descriptive adjectives. (p. 8)
READING	☐ I can identify topics and main ideas. (p. 9)
CRITICAL THINKING	☐ I can generate ideas with listing. (p. 12)
WRITING	☐ I can write simple sentences. (p. 13)
GRAMMAR	☐ I can use the present of *be* and simple present affirmative statements. (pp. 14 and 16)

OBJECTIVE ▶	☐ I can find information and ideas to write about my personality, appearance, and interests.

Education

VOCABULARY	recognizing word families
READING	scanning for names, dates, and times
CRITICAL THINKING	comparing and contrasting
WRITING	editing for capitalization and punctuation
GRAMMAR	simple present

Can students learn in different ways?

A. Discuss these questions with your classmates.

1. Look at the photo. What's unusual about where the students are learning? Could you learn in this place?

2. Most students study every day in a classroom with desks. What are some other ways to organize a school? What kind of school would you like to study in?

3. Do you know about any unusual schools? What makes them different?

B. Listen to *The Q Classroom* online. Then answer these questions.

1. Why does Marcus think students can learn in different ways?

2. Do the students agree about different kinds of learning? Explain.

3. Do you think learning in different ways is good? Why or why not?

iQ PRACTICE Go to the online discussion board to discuss the Unit Question with your classmates. *Practice > Unit 2 > Activity 1*

UNIT OBJECTIVE ▶ Read the article. Find information and ideas to write about a school.

Unusual Schools

You are going to read an article about unusual schools. Use the article to find information and ideas for your Unit Assignment.

PREVIEW THE READING

A. VOCABULARY Here are some words from the reading. Read the sentences. Then write each underlined word next to the correct definition.

A flood

1. I saw many <u>unusual</u> animals at the zoo.

2. My mother will go to <u>pick up</u> my sister after school.

3. In Hollywood, I saw a <u>famous</u> actor.

4. After the rain, there was a big <u>flood</u>.

5. The children <u>attend</u> a public school.

6. The workers on the <u>farm</u> are planting corn.

7. My mother cooks a lot of food. We can <u>feed</u> many teenagers at our house.

8. The cows were eating grass out in a <u>field</u>.

a. _attend_ *(verb)* to go to or be present at a place

b. _famous_ *(adjective)* known by many people

c. _farm_ *(noun)* land and buildings where people keep animals and grow plants for food

d. _feed_ *(verb)* to give food to a person or an animal

e. _Field_ (*noun*) a piece of land used for animals or for growing plants for food, usually surrounded by a fence, trees, etc.

f. _Flood_ (*noun*) when water covers the land

g. _pick up_ (*verb phrase*) to go to get someone or something

h. _unusual_ (*adjective*) something that does not often happen, or you do not often see

iQ PRACTICE Go online for more practice with vocabulary.
Practice > Unit 2 > Activities 2–3

B. PREVIEW Read the title of the article below. Read the captions under the photos. Where are these students studying?

C. QUICK WRITE What is your school like? Describe the place and how you feel when you are there. Write for five minutes. Remember to use this section for your Unit Assignment.

_____

_____

WORK WITH THE READING

🔊 **A. INVESTIGATE** Read the article. Find information about unusual schools.

Students in class on a boat

Unusual Schools

1   Do you like school? Or do you think school is boring? Maybe you want to go to a different kind of school. Some schools are very **unusual**.

2   In Argentina, one school is in a very interesting place. More than 2,000 children **attend** the River Plate Academy in Buenos Aires. Why is this school different? It is inside a large soccer stadium[1]. Sometimes the national soccer team of Argentina plays in this stadium. More than 70,000 people can watch a game here. **Famous** singers and bands play concerts in the stadium. Many of the students want to become soccer players.

3   The country of Bangladesh is near India. It rains a lot every year. This causes **floods**. It is difficult for people to travel because of all the water. As a result, in some places, there are special schools. These schools are on boats! The boats

[1] **stadium**: a place with seats around it where you can watch sports

Students enjoy the beautiful outdoors.

pick up students from their small towns. Then the students have class on the boat on the water. The students sit on wooden benches. The teacher uses a blackboard. The students could not go to school without the boats.

4   Do you like to be outside? Maybe you would like the Mountain School. This school is in the state of Vermont in the United States. Students at this school are 16 or 17 years old. They attend the Mountain School for just one term[2]. The students come from different parts of the United States. They live at the school. They work on the school's **farm** to help grow food. They **feed** the farm animals. Students also help clean the school. The students enjoy activities in the beautiful outdoors. They visit the nearby forests, **fields**, and rivers. On weekends, students play sports and games together. Or, like many students, they sleep late!

5   Are there too many rules at your school? You should try the Brooklyn Free School in New York. Students can choose any class they want. Students help make important decisions at this school. The students help make the school rules. Some students study independently[3]. Others decide to play or draw pictures. There are no tests, homework, or grades.

6   Is there anything unusual about your school? Why is it special?

[2] **term:** one of the periods of time which the academic year is divided into at some colleges and universities
[3] **independently:** without needing or wanting help

B. CATEGORIZE Read the statements. Write *T* (true) or *F* (false.) Write the paragraph number where you found the answer. Correct each false statement to make it true.

____ 1. An academy in Argentina is in a soccer stadium. Paragraph: ____

_____

____ 2. Famous singers play concerts at the stadium. Paragraph: ____

_____

____ 3. Many students at the River Plate Academy want to become basketball players. Paragraph: ____

_____

____ 4. There are many floods in Bangladesh because the weather is sunny. Paragraph: ____

_____

____ 5. Some students in Bangladesh have class on boats. Paragraph: ____

_____

____ 6. Students at the Mountain School work in a factory. Paragraph: ____

_____

____ 7. The Mountain School students help to clean the school. Paragraph: ____

_____

____ 8. At the Brooklyn Free School, students help make the rules. Paragraph: ____

_____

____ 9. Students at the Brooklyn Free School have many tests. Paragraph: ____

_____

C. APPLY Complete the statements. Use information from the article.

1. River Plate Academy is in the country of _____.

2. The academy is unusual because it is in a(n) _____.

3. In Bangladesh, some students go to school on _____.

4. They have special schools because of the problem with _____.

5. Students at the Mountain School like to be _____.

6. Students at that school work on a(n) _____.

7. At the Brooklyn Free School, students can _____ any class they want.

8. Students help make rules and important _____.

iQ PRACTICE Go online for additional reading and comprehension.
Practice › Unit 2 › Activity 4

BUILDING VOCABULARY Recognizing word families

Word families are groups of similar words. Word families can include nouns, verbs, and adjectives. Learn words in word families, and learn the part of speech of each word.

Noun	Verb	Adjective
help	help	helpful
teacher	teach	
student	study	studious

Do you need some **help**? (noun)
I can **help** you tomorrow. (verb)
My teacher is very **helpful**. (adjective)

A. IDENTIFY Label the underlined words. Write *N* (noun), *V* (verb), or *Adj* (adjective).

1. My teacher is a kind person. He is very <u>friendly</u> *Adj* with the <u>students</u> *N*.

2. My cousin <u>helps</u> me with my <u>difficult</u> homework. He's <u>helpful</u>.

3. My brother is very <u>studious</u>. He <u>studies</u> about four hours every night. He is very <u>intelligent</u>.

4. I <u>study</u> at a math <u>academy</u> on Saturdays. I <u>enjoy</u> the classes there.

5. Our <u>academic</u> year starts in September.

6. For me, the most <u>enjoyable</u> part of the day is lunch.

B. EXTEND Complete the chart with words from Activity A. (An *X* means that the word doesn't exist or that you don't need to know it.)

	Noun	Verb	Adjective
1.	academy	X	academic
2.	difficulty	X	
3.	X		enjoyable
4.	friend	X	friendly
5.	help		
6.	intelligence	X	
7.		study	

iQ PRACTICE Go online for more practice with recognizing word families. *Practice > Unit 2 > Activity 5*

READING SKILL Scanning for names, dates, and times

You **scan** a text to find information quickly. When you scan, move your eyes quickly over the text. Only look for the information you need.

Use these techniques to scan a reading.

- To find **names** of people or places, look for capital letters.
☐ Brian, New York, Egypt

- To find **days** or **months**, look for capital letters.
☐ Monday, October

- To find **dates** or **times**, look for numbers and abbreviations (like *a.m.* and *p.m.*).
☐ in 2009, at 8:30 a.m., 5 hours

A. IDENTIFY Scan the two paragraphs. Complete these steps.

1. Underline the names of the countries.
2. Circle the number of days in the school year.
3. Put two lines under the times of day and months of the year.

Schools in Germany

Jens lives in Germany. He says, "We start school at 7:30 in the morning. That's too early for me! Classes end at 1:30 p.m., so our school day is only six hours. Our school day is pretty short, but our school year is really long. The term begins in September and lasts until July. We take a short vacation in the summer—about six weeks. We study for 200 days each year. But I enjoy school. I study with my good friends, and we learn a lot of interesting things. I think our time in school is about right."

Students in Germany

Schools Around the World

Around the world, students spend different numbers of days in school. For example, students in France study for 170 days each year, but in Australia, the school year is 200 days long. The number of hours each day is also different from country to country. The school day in France and Kenya is eight hours long and lasts from 8:00 a.m. to 4:00 p.m. But students in France get a two-hour break for lunch, so they only study for six hours a day. Students in Spain start school at 8:00 a.m. and attend class until 3:00 p.m. Their school day is seven hours long.

Students in Kenya

B. IDENTIFY Answer the questions.

1. How long is the school year in France? _____

2. How long is the school day in Germany? _____

3. Which country has the shortest school year? _____

4. Which countries begin school at 8:00 a.m.? _____

5. Which country has school for seven hours a day? _____

 CRITICAL THINKING STRATEGY

Comparing and contrasting

One way to think about new ideas is to compare items. When you **compare and contrast**, you see the way that items are the same and the way they are different. For example, to compare and contrast elementary school and high school, we ask, *How are they the same?*

⎡ Students must attend for many years.
⎣ Students sit in a classroom.

Then we ask, *How are they different?*

⎡ In elementary school, you have the same classes every day. In high school, you may have different classes.

⎣ In elementary school, there isn't a lot of homework. In high school, students must do a lot of homework.

iQ PRACTICE Go online to watch the Critical Thinking Video and check your comprehension. *Practice › Unit 2 › Activity 6*

C. APPLY Read the descriptions. Then decide if the schools are being compared or contrasted. Write *S* (same) or *D* (different).

____ 1. The River Plate Academy and the Bangladesh boat schools are in unusual places.

____ 2. River Plate students learn in a stadium. The Bangladeshi students learn on boats.

____ 3. Students at the Mountain School help clean the school. Students at the Brooklyn Free School can choose their classes.

____ 4. In elementary school, you usually have the same teacher all day. In high school, you have different teachers.

iQ PRACTICE Go online for more practice with scanning for names, dates, and times. *Practice › Unit 2 › Activity 7*

WORK WITH THE VIDEO

A. PREVIEW Where do you like to study? Do you do your homework at school, in your room, or in a library?

VIDEO VOCABULARY

bell (n.) a metal thing that makes a sound when something hits or touches it

subject (n.) something you study at school, college, or university

experiment (n.) a scientific test that you do to find out what will happen or to see if something is true

healthy (adj.) helping to make or keep you well

coach (n.) a person who trains a person or team in a sport

iQ RESOURCES Go online to watch the video about Millfield School in England. *Resources > Video > Unit 2 > Unit Video*

B. IDENTIFY Watch the video two or three times. Then circle the correct answers.

1. Tim studies *three / four* subjects.

2. The students eat *lunch / dinner* at the school.

3. Many of the students at Millfield School like to *study science / play sports*.

4. Tim plays tennis for about *one hour / two hours*.

5. Tim does his homework in *the library / his room*.

C. DISCUSS Discuss the questions in a group.

1. Tim likes studying science. What subjects do you like to study?

2. Tim likes to play tennis. What sports do you like to play?

3. Some of the students at Millfield live at the school. Would you like to live at your school? Why or why not?

WRITE WHAT YOU THINK

A. DISCUSS Discuss these questions with a partner or in a group.

1. Would you like to attend an unusual school? Which one?

2. Would you like to have class outside?

3. Do you think summer vacations are too long or too short?

B. SYNTHESIZE Choose and write the number of one question from Activity A. Then write a response. Look back at your Quick Write on page 23. Think about what you learned.

Question: ____

My response: _____

_____

_____

WRITING

OBJECTIVE ▶

At the end of this unit, you are going to write about a school. Your sentences will include information from the reading, the unit video, and your own ideas.

WRITING SKILL **Editing for capitalization and punctuation**

When you write, check for correct **capitalization** and **punctuation**.

Capitalization rules

- Capitalize the first word in a statement or question.

  ⌐ I have a short study period every afternoon.
  ⌐ Do young students usually wear uniforms?

- Capitalize proper nouns: the names of people, places, and languages.

  ⌐ My name is Tim. I'm from San Diego. I attend City College. I speak English.

- Capitalize the days of the week and the months of the year.

  ⌐ Classes start on Monday, October 12.

- Capitalize I, even if it does not begin a sentence.

  ⌐ My friend and I went to class.

Punctuation rules

- End every statement with a period (.).

  ⌐ The high school has difficult academic classes.

- End every question with a question mark (?).

  ⌐ How much vacation time do you have every year?

iQ **RESOURCES** **Go online to watch the Writing Skill Video.**
Resources > Video > Unit 2 > Writing Skill Video

IDENTIFY Correct the errors in capitalization and punctuation.

1. are there many students in your classes

2. my exam is on february 3

3. the team practices every saturday for three hours

4. my classmate is from italy

5. our new teacher is from cairo, egypt

6. when is your lunch break

7. do you study in the library or at home

8. my cousin attends hong kong university

9. nour and majda both speak arabic

10. i work at super burger, and i wear a uniform

iQ PRACTICE Go online for more practice with editing for capitalization and punctuation. *Practice > Unit 2 > Activity 8*

GRAMMAR Simple present

TIP FOR SUCCESS

Remember to use the base verb + *-s* or *-es* after *he*, *she*, and *it*.

Use the **simple present** to describe or ask about habits, facts, or feelings.

Affirmative statements

subject	verb	
I / You / We / They	**attend**	school on Saturday.
He / She	**attends**	

Negative statements

subject	*do/does + not*	verb	
I / You / We / They	**do not** **don't**	**take**	a lunch break.
He / She	**does not** **doesn't**		

Yes/No questions

do/does	subject	verb	
Do	you	**study**	hard?
Does	she	**have**	many friends?

Short answers

yes	no
Yes, I **do**.	No, I **don't**.
Yes, she **does**.	No, she **doesn't**.

Information questions

wh- word	*do/does*	subject	verb	
What	**do**	you	**talk**	about?
Where	**does**	he	**live**?	
When	**does**	she	**call**	you?

Answers

We **talk** about school.

He **lives** in Oman.

She **calls** me after dinner.

A. CREATE Complete each sentence to make it true for you. Use the correct form of the verb in parentheses. Use the negative (*don't/doesn't*) if necessary.

1. I _____*don't go*_____ to school Monday through Friday. (go)

2. At my school, students _____ uniforms. (wear)

3. I _____ a one-hour lunch break. (have)

4. A typical class _____ about 50 minutes. (last)

5. My best friend _____ my school. (attend)

6. I _____ sports after school. (play)

7. My English teacher _____ us a test every Friday. (give)

B. COMPOSE Write questions with *Do* or *Does*. Answer the questions. Then ask and answer the questions with a partner.

1. you and your friends / study together

   Do you and your friends study together? No, we don't.

2. your teacher / talk to you about college

   _____

3. your best friend / speak English well

   _____

4. you / like academic courses

   _____

5. your school / have a vacation soon

   _____

6. you / enjoy math classes

   _____

7. your teacher / give a lot of homework

   _____

C. APPLY Read about Rika. There are six errors. Correct them. The first one is done for you.

> have
> Do you ~~has~~ a busy academic life?
>
> Yes, I do. My life at school is very busy. My school start at 7:00 every day. Classes last until 2:30 p.m. We not have a long lunch break. We have just 30 minutes, so we don't have much time to relax. We eat lunch in the cafeteria. I enjoy my classes, but they are difficult. My teachers are very helpful. My science teacher often help me after class. In the afternoon, I play soccer. Our school have an excellent soccer team. That is the best part of my day. At night, I does homework.

Rika

D. COMPOSE Write questions. Then answer the questions.

1. When / Rika's school / start?

   When does Rika's school start?

   It starts at 7:00.

2. Where / Rika / eat lunch?

   _____

   _____

3. When / Rika's science teacher / help her?

   _____

   _____

iQ PRACTICE Go online for more practice with the simple present.
Practice > Unit 2 > Activities 9–10

UNIT ASSIGNMENT
OBJECTIVE ▶

Give information about a school

In this assignment, you are going to write about a school. Think about the Unit Question, "Can students learn in different ways?" Use the reading, the unit video, and your work in this unit. Look at the Self-Assessment checklist on page 36.

iQ PRACTICE   Go online to the Writing Tutor to read a writing model.
Practice > Unit 2 > Activity 11

A. BRAINSTORM What words do we use to talk about schools? Write them in the chart. Then share your ideas with a partner.

Schedule/Time	Classes	Homework
busy	large	difficult

WRITING TIP
Check your prepositions.
• Use *for* + amount of time (*for six hours*).
• Use *at* + specific time (*at 3:00*).
• Use *on* + day of the week (*on Monday*).
• Use *in* + month (*in July*).
• Use *from . . . to* with two times (*from 8:00 to 3:00*; *from January to June*).

B. WRITE Answer the questions about the school. Write complete sentences. Use your brainstorm chart to help you.

1. What kind of school are you writing about?

2. Where do students have classes?

3. How long is the summer vacation?

4. How long is the school day?

5. What do you like about the school?

6. What do you dislike about going to school?

7. How much time do students spend on homework each night?

8. Do you think students can learn in different ways?

iQ RESOURCES   Go online to download and complete the outline for your sentences. *Resources > Writing Tools > Unit 2 > Outline*

iQ PRACTICE   Go online to the Writing Tutor to write your assignment.
Practice > Unit 2 > Activity 12

iQ RESOURCES   Go online to download the peer review worksheet.
Resources > Writing Tools > Unit 2 > Peer Review Worksheet

C. REVISE Review your sentences with a partner. Read your partner's sentences. Then use the peer review worksheet. Discuss the review with your partner.

D. EDIT AND REWRITE Complete the Self-Assessment checklist. Make final changes to your sentences. Be prepared to hand in your work or discuss it in class.

SELF-ASSESSMENT	Yes	No
Does every sentence start with a capital letter?	☐	☐
Does every sentence have a subject and a verb?	☐	☐
Are months and days of the week capitalized?	☐	☐
Does every sentence end with a period?	☐	☐
Check your verbs. Do you use the correct form of the simple present?	☐	☐
Do you use vocabulary from this unit?	☐	☐

E. REFLECT Discuss these questions with a partner or group.

1. What is something new you learned in this unit?

2. Look back at the Unit Question—Can students learn in different ways? Is your answer different now than when you started the unit? If yes, how is it different?

iQ PRACTICE Go to the online discussion board to discuss the questions.
Practice > Unit 2 > Activity 13

TRACK YOUR SUCCESS

iQ PRACTICE Go online to check the words and phrases you have learned in this unit. *Practice > Unit 2 > Activity 14*

Check (✓) the skills you learned. If you need more work on a skill, refer to the page(s) in parentheses.

VOCABULARY	☐ I can recognize word families. (p. 25)
READING	☐ I can scan for names, dates, and times. (p. 26)
CRITICAL THINKING	☐ I can compare and contrast. (p. 28)
WRITING	☐ I can edit my writing for capitalization and punctuation. (p. 31)
GRAMMAR	☐ I can use the simple present in statements and questions. (p. 32)

OBJECTIVE ▶ ☐ I can find information and ideas to write about a school.

3

Cultural Studies

READING	review: scanning for information
VOCABULARY	using the dictionary
GRAMMAR	adjectives and adverbs
WRITING	writing complete sentences
CRITICAL THINKING	choosing a writing topic

When do we eat special foods?

A. Work with a partner. Why do you usually eat? Check (✓) the boxes. Then discuss your ideas with your classmates.

I eat because . . .

☐ I'm hungry.

☐ it's time for a meal.

☐ it's fun to do with friends.

☐ I like to be with my family.

B. Listen to *The Q Classroom* online. Then answer these questions.

1. When do the students eat special foods? Complete the chart with the ideas from the box.

| weekends | barbecues in the summer |
| ~~holidays~~ | special celebrations |

	Event
Sophy	holidays
Yuna	
Marcus	
Felix	

2. Look at the photo. What special foods do you eat at celebrations?

iQ PRACTICE Go to the online discussion board to discuss the Unit Question with your classmates. *Practice > Unit 3 > Activity 1*

UNIT OBJECTIVE

Read the article from a textbook. Find information and ideas to describe the people, food, and activities at a celebration.

READING

OBJECTIVE ▶

Celebrating with Food

You are going to read an article from a textbook. The article is about celebrations of food around the world. Use the article to find information and ideas for your Unit Assignment.

PREVIEW THE READING

VOCABULARY SKILL REVIEW

In Unit 2, you learned about word families. As you learn new vocabulary, remember to study other parts of speech in the same word family. In Activity A, how can you change the words *celebrate* and *prepare* to nouns? Use your dictionary.

A. VOCABULARY Here are some words from the reading. Look at the photos and read the descriptions (A–D). Then write each underlined word next to the correct definition.

(A) I like <u>fresh</u> vegetables, not canned or frozen ones. I enjoy <u>delicious</u> vegetables from my garden—tomatoes, peppers, and lettuce.

(B) Weddings are a <u>special</u> time for people around the world. Most people <u>celebrate</u> their marriages by having a large party for their friends and family.

A traditional Japanese wedding

(C) Cookouts are <u>popular</u> for summer holidays. Families <u>prepare</u> grilled beef or chicken, potato salad, and fresh watermelon.

TIP FOR SUCCESS

Event is a general term for something that happens. Usually an event is planned. You can have a *family event*, a *special event*, a *sports event*, or *an historical event*. *Event* is a very common word in academic English.

(D) Farmers <u>grow</u> a lot of strawberries in my area. Every summer, our school has a festival with strawberry sundaes. It is my favorite <u>event</u> of the summer.

1. _____ *(adjective)* not usual or ordinary

2. _____ *(adjective)* not frozen or in a can

3. _____ *(verb)* to make (a dish or a meal)

4. _____ (verb) to do something to show that you are happy because it is a special day

5. _____ (adjective) liked by a lot of people

6. _____ (noun) something important that happens

7. _____ (verb) to plant something in the ground and take care of it

8. _____ (adjective) very good to eat

iQ PRACTICE Go online for more practice with the vocabulary.
Practice > Unit 3 > Activities 2–3

B. PREVIEW Look quickly over the article below. Check (✓) the true statements.

☐ 1. The topic of this article is food in the United States.

☐ 2. There is a paragraph about a garlic festival.

☐ 3. There is a paragraph about a type of fish called herring.

☐ 4. The article describes food festivals in different countries.

☐ 5. The topic of this article is unusual vegetables.

Garlic

C. QUICK WRITE Think about the food that you like to eat. Answer these questions with complete sentences. Use this section for your Unit Assignment.

1. What is your favorite food? _____

2. Who prepares the food? _____

3. When do you eat it? _____

Herring

WORK WITH THE READING

 A. INVESTIGATE Read the textbook article. Find information about special foods.

Celebrating with Food

The Gilroy Garlic Festival

1   People around the world **celebrate special events** with food. People enjoy special food at weddings, on holidays, and on birthdays. Some people also celebrate food with festivals! These festivals are usually once a year. They can be fun and unusual, but they are always **delicious**.

2   The Gilroy Garlic Festival in Gilroy, California, is in July. It is a very big event. Gilroy **grows** a lot of garlic. Every year over 4,000 people make food for over 100,000 visitors. Cooks **prepare** many different dishes with garlic. You can even buy garlic popcorn and garlic ice cream. Visitors also enjoy listening to music.

3   The International White Truffle Fair is in October in Alba, Italy. Truffles are delicious with pasta or rice. They are very expensive. In fact, they sometimes cost $3,000 per pound (0.45 kilograms)!

White truffles

Selling herring at the Baltic Herring Festival

4   The Baltic Herring Festival in Helsinki, Finland, is over 270 years old. The festival celebrates a **popular** fish, the herring. For one week in October, fishermen sell fried herring, herring soup, herring sandwiches, and herring pizza. You can buy **fresh** herring, too, and make your own dish. You can also buy handmade gifts and warm winter clothes.

5   Finally, the Cooper's Hill Cheese-Rolling and Wake is a very popular festival. This event in Gloucestershire, UK, is over 200 years old. The organizers buy a big piece of cheese. It weighs over 6 pounds (2.72 kilograms). They drop the cheese down a hill. People watch as young men and women run after the cheese. Ambulances wait at the bottom of the hill because people sometimes hurt themselves. Cheese-rolling is dangerous, but it is a lot of fun.

The small, white object bouncing down the center of the hill is a wheel of cheese.

B. IDENTIFY Write the correct paragraph number next to each main idea.

1. There is a lot of garlic in Gilroy, California. Paragraph: ____

2. The cheese-rolling in Gloucestershire is a popular event. Paragraph: ____

3. People in some regions of the world like to celebrate the food they produce. Paragraph: ____

4. The Baltic Herring Festival is an old event. Paragraph: ____

5. You can find truffles in the Alba region of Italy. Paragraph: ____

C. CATEGORIZE Read the statements. Write *T* (true) or *F* (false). Write the paragraph number where you found the answer. Then correct each false statement to make it true.

____ 1. Only people in Italy like to celebrate holidays with special food. Paragraph: ____

_____

____ 2. Special festivals with food usually happen once a month. Paragraph: ____

_____

____ 3. The Gilroy Garlic Festival has both food and music. Paragraph: ____

_____

____ 4. You can get popcorn with garlic at the Gilroy Garlic Festival. Paragraph: ____

_____

____ 5. People eat a lot of chocolate at the International White Truffle Fair. Paragraph: ____

_____

____ 6. Truffles are not very expensive. Paragraph: ____

_____

____ 7. A herring festival is held each year in Oslo, Norway. Paragraph: ____

_____

____ 8. You can only buy fish at the herring festival. Paragraph: ____

_____

____ 9. People roll small pieces of cheese down Cooper's Hill. Paragraph: ____

_____

____10. People are sometimes hurt at the cheese-rolling. Paragraph: ____

_____

D. APPLY Complete the statements. Use information from the article.

1. People like to _____ holidays with special food.

2. Special festivals can be found in many different _____.

3. At the Gilroy Garlic Festival there is food and _____.

4. Cooks _____ and sell many kinds of food with garlic.

5. The International White Truffle Fair in Alba, Italy, takes place in the month of _____.

6. Truffles are very _____.

7. The Baltic Herring Festival is more than _____ years old.

8. If you want to cook your own food, you can buy _____ herring.

9. At Cooper's Hill, people run down the hill after the _____.

10. People sometimes get hurt, so there are _____ at the bottom of the cheese-rolling hill.

iQ PRACTICE Go online for additional reading and comprehension.
Practice ⟩ Unit 3 ⟩ Activity 4

READING SKILL REVIEW Scanning for information

Remember: you **scan** a text to find information quickly. Only look for the information you need. To find information about a person or place, look for capital letters. You can also scan for a specific word. Review the Reading Skill in Unit 2, page 26.

IDENTIFY Read each question. Then scan the reading to find the underlined word. Answer the question.

1. What product does the area around the town of <u>Gilroy</u> produce?

   _____

2. How much can one <u>pound</u> of truffles cost? _____

3. In what <u>month</u> is the Baltic Herring Festival? _____

4. Why are there <u>ambulances</u> at the Gloucestershire event? _____

   _____

5. "<u>Delicious</u>" is one way to describe food festivals. What are two other words used to describe them? _____

6. How many <u>visitors</u> attend the Gilroy Garlic Festival? _____

You can build your vocabulary by **using the dictionary**. Look at the dictionary entry.

> fruit ⚲ /frut/ *noun* [*count, noncount*]
>
> ❶ **PRONUNCIATION**
> The word **fruit** sounds like **boot**.
>
> the part of a plant or tree that holds the seeds.
> Oranges and apples are types of **fruit**: *Would
> you like a **a piece of fruit**?* ♦ *"Would you like **some**
> **fruit**?" "Yes please – I'll have a pear."*

Use the dictionary entry to learn new words. In this definition for *fruit,* you can learn other important words: *plant, tree,* and *seeds.* You learn that oranges, apples, and pears are types of fruit. In addition, many learners' dictionaries have color illustrations to show vocabulary.

All dictionary entries adapted from the *Oxford American Dictionary for Learners of English* © Oxford University Press 2011

TIP FOR SUCCESS

Learn words to describe food: *delicious, fresh, bitter, spicy, salty, sweet,* and *sour.* These adjectives answer the question, "How does it taste?"

A. IDENTIFY Look at the dictionary entries. Answer the questions.

1.
> meal ⚲ /mil/ *noun* [*count*]
> food that you eat at a certain time of the day:
> *What's your favorite meal of the day?* ♦ *We **had** a
> nice **meal** in that restaurant.*
>
> **Culture**
> ■ **Breakfast, lunch,** and **dinner** are the usual
>   meals of the day.
> ■ We do not usually use "a" with the names
>   of meals: *Let's **have** lunch together
>   tomorrow.*

a. What are three meals? _____

b. Write a sentence with the word *meal.* _____

_____

2.
> veg·e·ta·ble ⚲ /'vɛdʒtəbl/ *noun* [*count*]
> a plant or part of a plant that we eat: *The
> students grow vegetables such as cabbages,
> beans, and carrots.*

a. What are three other vegetables? _____

_____

b. Write a sentence with the word *vegetable.* _____

_____

B. CATEGORIZE Make a food chart. Add the words from the box, and then add more foods. If necessary, use a dictionary. Compare your chart with your partner.

apples	beans	cheese	grapes	milk	potatoes
bananas	beef	chicken	lobster	onion	shrimp

Fruit	Vegetables	Meat	Seafood	Dairy
apples				

iQ PRACTICE Go online for more practice with using the dictionary.
Practice > Unit 3 > Activity 5

WORK WITH THE VIDEO

A. PREVIEW What festivals or holidays do you celebrate? Do you eat special food?

VIDEO VOCABULARY

festival (n.) a time when people celebrate something

roll (v.) to make something into a long, round shape or the shape of a ball

pancake (n.) a very thin, round thing that you eat

dessert (n.) something sweet that you eat at the end of a meal

fireworks (n.) things that explode with bright lights and loud noises, used for entertainment

iQ RESOURCES Go online to watch the video about Chinese New Year.
Resources > Video > Unit 3 > Unit Video

B. IDENTIFY Watch the video two or three times. Then complete the sentences with the words from the box.

dessert	festival	home	presents	restaurant

1. Chinese New Year is a special _____.

2. Some families like to stay at _____ and cook.

3. Other families like to go out and eat in a _____.

4. At the end of a meal, people enjoy a sweet _____.

5. Children like to receive _____.

C. DISCUSS Discuss the questions in a group.

1. When do you give gifts to people? What kinds of gifts are popular?

2. Do you like to eat at home with your family or in a restaurant?

3. What food reminds you of home?

WRITE WHAT YOU THINK

A. DISCUSS Ask and answer these questions with a partner. Look back at your Quick Write on page 41. Think about what you learned.

1. What is your favorite celebration?

2. When do you usually have this celebration?

3. What special foods do you eat? Why?

4. What is your favorite food at this celebration?

B. SYNTHESIZE Think about the reading and the unit video as you discuss these questions. Then choose and write the number of one question. Then write 3–5 sentences.

1. What kind of food is very special to you?

2. How would you describe your favorite celebration?

Question: ____

_____

_____

_____

_____

WRITING

OBJECTIVE ▶

At the end of this unit, you are going to write about the people, food, and activities at a celebration. Your sentences will include information from the reading, the unit video, and your own ideas.

GRAMMAR Adjectives and adverbs

Adjectives describe nouns (people, places, or things).

- An adjective can come after the verb *be*. It describes the subject.

subject (noun)	*be*	adjective
Ice cream	is	**cold**.
The sandwiches	are	**huge**.

- An adjective can come before a noun. It describes the noun.

	adjective	noun
This is an	**unusual**	wedding.
I'm celebrating a	**special**	day.

- There are no singular or plural adjectives.

✓   Correct: **popular**

✗   Incorrect: populars

- Do not use an article (*the*, *a*, or *an*) before an adjective with no noun.

✓   Correct: This is a **delicious** meal. This is **delicious**.

✗   Incorrect: This is a delicious.

Adverbs can describe adjectives.

The pizza is **very hot**.   Our dinner is **quite expensive**.

The vegetables are **really fresh**.   She is **extremely hungry**.

The food is **very good**.   It's a **very popular** festival.

iQ RESOURCES   Go online to watch the Grammar Skill Video.
Resources > Video > Unit 3 > Grammar Skill Video

Pizza

A. IDENTIFY Circle the adverb and underline the adjective in each sentence.

1. The garlic festival is (very) popular.
2. This is a really big pizza.
3. The cheese is quite expensive.
4. Leila's recipe is really good.
5. The tea is really hot!

6. These are extremely fresh vegetables.
7. Our town has a very special festival.
8. This is a very small sandwich.
9. That is an extremely big truffle.
10. They enjoy really delicious food.

B. IDENTIFY There is one error in each sentence. Find the errors and correct them.

1. It's a nice really garden.
2. This is a good dinner extremely.
3. Jim's vegetables are expensives.
4. The event is quite a popular.
5. This food is bad extremely.
6. This noodle soup is a delicious.
7. Everything on the menu is expensive quite.
8. The summer festivals are very bigs.

Pho ga, or Vietnamese chicken noodle soup

iQ PRACTICE Go online for more practice with adjectives and adverbs. *Practice › Unit 3 › Activity 6*

iQ PRACTICE Go online for the Grammar Expansion: Using *more* and *less* with adjectives. *Practice › Unit 3 › Activity 7*

WRITING SKILL **Writing complete sentences**

Every **complete sentence** needs a **subject** and a **verb**. The subject is a noun or pronoun. It answers the question, "Who or what is the sentence about?" The **verb** is the action. It answers the question, "What does the subject do, think, or feel?"

I prepare dinner every day.
subject verb

Usually my dinners are delicious.
subject verb

My friends like to go to cafes.
subject verb

Right now, they are at a cafe.
subject verb

The subject can be singular or plural. *Singular* means "one." *Plural* means "more than one."

Singular	Plural
dish	dishes
backpack	backpacks
John	John and Mary
I	we
you (1 person)	you (more than 1 person)
he, she, it	they

Always make your subject and verb agree.

✓　　Correct: **I like** oranges.　　← Subject and verb agree.

✓　　Correct: **He likes** oranges.　　← Subject and verb agree.

✗　Incorrect: He like oranges.　　← Subject and verb do not agree.

A. APPLY Add a subject (*he, she, it*, or *they*) or the verb *be* to each sentence.

1. My brother ^is^ a student in a cooking program.

2. Is a very difficult book.

3. There delicious dishes on this menu.

4. Are very good cookies.

5. Is an excellent baker.

6. Kate at the cafe this afternoon.

7. I rarely eat seafood because it usually very expensive.

8. Hatem likes to eat in restaurants because doesn't like cooking.

B. IDENTIFY Correct the incorrect verb in each sentence.

1. Sam ~~go~~ *goes* to the cafeteria after class.

2. Mary have a new job as a waitress.

3. They loves to eat ice cream in the park.

4. Hassan prepare coffee every morning.

5. I are at the same table as my friends.

6. Isabel don't like baking cakes.

7. We like eating chicken on Saturdays, and we usually has steak on Sundays.

C. APPLY Complete the paragraph. Use the correct verb forms.

For Chinese New Year, we celebrate with traditional foods. First, we usually

____eat_____ round dumplings. These dumplings
　　　　1. (eat)

_____ small pieces of meat wrapped in a covering. Then we
　　　　2. (be)

_____ to eat duck. It _____ a lot like chicken.
　　　　3. (like)　　　　　　　　　　　　　4. (taste)

I _____ eating long noodles. We also _____ fish.
　　　　5. (enjoy)　　　　　　　　　　　　　　　　　　6. (prepare)

The fish _____ a wish for a happy year ahead. Sometimes people
　　　　　　　7. (be)

_____ a special vegetarian dish. This dish _____
　　　　8. (eat)　　　　　　　　　　　　　　　　　　　　9. (have)

only vegetables in it. After seven days we enjoy a special salad. Everyone also

_____ cake. The cake _____ very popular.
　　　　10. (eat)　　　　　　　　　　　　　11. (be)

D. COMPOSE Write sentences about yourself with the words in parentheses.
Change the verb if necessary. Label the subject *S* and the verb *V* in
each sentence.

　　　　　　　　　　　　S　　V
1. (enjoy going out) _I enjoy going out for breakfast._____

2. (don't like to eat) _____

3. (like to eat) _____

4. (enjoy preparing) _____

5. (like to celebrate) _____

E. APPLY Put the words in the correct order to make sentences.

1. They / delicious / prepare / pizzas

_____

2. soup / The / is / hot / extremely

_____

3. Mr. Adams / garden / grows / tomatoes / large / very / in his

_____

4. fresh / food / really / The / is

_____

5. Everyone / festival / enjoys celebrating / the popular / at

_____

6. like / ice cream / good / We

_____

7. The TV show / funny / very / is

_____

8. likes / hot / James / tea

_____

9. Lisa / special / prepares / food / for the holiday

_____

iQ PRACTICE Go online for more practice with writing complete sentences.
Practice > Unit 3 > Activity 8

UNIT ASSIGNMENT

OBJECTIVE ▶

Describe the people, food, and activities at a celebration

In this assignment, you are going to write about the people, food, and activities at a celebration. Think about the Unit Question, "When do we eat special foods?" Use the reading, the unit video, and your work in this unit. Look at the Self-Assessment checklist on page 54.

iQ PRACTICE Go online to the Writing Tutor to read a writing model.
Practice > Unit 3 > Activity 9

A. BRAINSTORM Think of two different celebrations or special meals to write about. Write them on the lines below. Then list ideas about each one. For example, list the foods, the people, and the activities.

1. Celebration or special meal 1: _____

_____

_____

2. Celebration or special meal 2: _____

_____

_____

 CRITICAL THINKING STRATEGY

Choosing a writing topic

Often you have to **choose a topic for a writing assignment**. Choosing a topic is an important first step. One way to do this is to write down two topics. Then quickly list ideas about each one.

For example, here are two topics for an assignment to write about a special celebration. Each topic has a list of ideas.

Birthday: sing song; eat cake; open presents
Wedding: watch wedding; greet bride and groom; eat special foods

After listing ideas, choose the best topic. Think about what you know about each topic. How much can you write about the topic? Then ask yourself these questions:

- Which topic is more interesting to you? Why?
- Which topic do you have more details about?
- Which topic answers the assignment question best?

After asking yourself these questions, you can choose the best topic. Your topic should be interesting and should have many details to write about. Also, your topic should answer the assignment question.

iQ PRACTICE Go online to watch the Critical Thinking Video and check your comprehension. *Practice ⟩ Unit 3 ⟩ Activity 10*

B. EVALUATE Look at the two topics you brainstormed in Activity A. With a partner, discuss the questions about your topics.

1. Which topic is more interesting to you? Why?
2. Which topic do you have more details about?
3. Which topic answers the assignment question best?
4. Which topic is the best? Why?

C. CREATE Look at the categories in the idea map. Then draw an idea map for your topic. Complete the map with words about a special meal or celebration. Then explain your map to a partner.

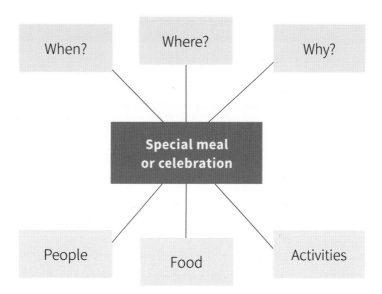

WRITING TIP

Answer these questions when describing something: *Who? What? When? Where? Why? How?* This will add information to your description.

D. WRITE Answer the questions. Use complete sentences. Use your idea map to help you.

1. What is the special meal or celebration?

2. When does it happen?

3. What do you need to do before the meal?

4. Do you enjoy preparing the food? Why or why not?

5. Where do you have the meal?

6. Who comes to the celebration?

7. What are the main dishes?

8. Why is the food special?

9. Which food do you love eating?

10. Which food do you not like? Why?

iQ RESOURCES Go online to download and complete the outline for your description. *Resources > Writing Tools > Unit 3 > Outline*

iQ PRACTICE Go online to the Writing Tutor to write your assignment. *Practice > Unit 3 > Activity 11*

iQ RESOURCES Go online to download the peer review worksheet. *Resources > Writing Tools > Unit 3 > Peer Review Worksheet*

E. REVISE Review your sentences with a partner. Read your partner's sentences. Then use the peer review worksheet. Discuss the review with your partner.

F. EDIT AND REWRITE Complete the Self-Assessment checklist. Make final changes to your sentences. Be prepared to hand in your work or discuss it in class.

SELF-ASSESSMENT	Yes	No
Does every sentence have a subject and a verb?	☐	☐
Do your subjects and verbs agree with each other?	☐	☐
Do you use adverbs and adjectives to add more information?	☐	☐
Do you use vocabulary from the unit?	☐	☐
Does every sentence start with a capital letter and end with a period?	☐	☐

G. REFLECT Discuss these questions with a partner or group.

1. What is something new you learned in this unit?

2. Look back at the Unit Question—When do we eat special foods? Is your answer different now than when you started the unit? If yes, how is it different?

iQ PRACTICE Go to the online discussion board to discuss the questions. *Practice > Unit 3 > Activity 12*

TRACK YOUR SUCCESS

iQ PRACTICE Go online to check the words and phrases you have learned in this unit. *Practice › Unit 3 › Activity 13*

Check (✓) the skills and strategies you learned. If you need more work on a skill, refer to the page(s) in parentheses.

READING	☐ I can scan for information. (p. 44)
VOCABULARY	☐ I can use the dictionary to build my vocabulary. (p. 45)
GRAMMAR	☐ I can use adjectives and adverbs. (p. 48)
WRITING	☐ I can write complete sentences. (p. 49)
CRITICAL THINKING	☐ I can choose a writing topic. (p. 52)

OBJECTIVE ▶ ☐ I can find information and ideas to describe the people, food, and activities at a celebration.

Sociology

4

CRITICAL THINKING	classifying
VOCABULARY	using verb + noun collocations
READING	underlining and highlighting
WRITING	capitalizing proper nouns
GRAMMAR	subject and object pronouns

How do you have fun?

A. Check (✓) the activities you enjoy. Put an *X* by activities you don't enjoy. Then compare with a partner.

☐ cooking   ☐ watching TV

☐ playing sports   ☐ telling funny stories

☐ going to the beach   ☐ watching sports

☐ playing games   ☐ going out to eat

B. Listen to *The Q Classroom* online. Then answer these questions.

1. How does each student have fun?

2. Which student do you agree with? Why?

iQ PRACTICE Go to the online discussion board to discuss the Unit Question with your classmates. *Practice ⟩ Unit 4 ⟩ Activity 1*

UNIT OBJECTIVE

Read the Web posts. Find information and ideas to write about how you have fun with your friends.

READING

OBJECTIVE ▶

No Money? Have Fun Anyway!

You are going to read Web posts about fun things to do without much money. Use the posts to find information and ideas for your Unit Assignment.

PREVIEW THE READING

A. VOCABULARY Here are some words from the reading. Read the definitions. Then complete the sentences.

> **cost** *(verb)* 🔑 to have the price of
>
> **guess** *(verb)* 🔑 to give an answer when you do not know if it is right
>
> **idea** *(noun)* 🔑 a plan or new thought
>
> **invite** *(verb)* 🔑 to ask someone to come to a party, to your home, etc.
>
> **nature** *(noun)* 🔑 OPAL plants and animals
>
> **program** *(noun)* 🔑 something on television or radio
>
> **sightseeing** *(noun)* visiting interesting buildings and places as a tourist
>
> **spend** *(verb)* 🔑 to pay money for something

🔑 Oxford 3000™ words   **OPAL** Oxford Phrasal Academic Lexicon

1. My friends and I enjoy _____ when we travel to new cities.

2. I like to hike in the mountains because I enjoy _____.

3. Toshi wants to _____ us to come over for dinner.

4. I saw a famous person today. Can you _____ her name?

5. There is an interesting science _____ on TV tonight.

6. These shoes _____ $70.

7. I have a great _____ for my mother's birthday present.

8. I _____ about $20 a week on coffee.

VOCABULARY SKILL REVIEW

In Unit 3, you learned to read examples in a dictionary entry. What example do you think the dictionary might give for the word *nature*?

B. APPLY Work with a partner. Ask and answer these questions.

1. How much do you spend each week on coffee or tea?

2. Do you like to relax in nature? Where do you go?

3. Where do you like to go sightseeing?

4. Can you guess my middle name?

5. What is your favorite TV program? Why do you like it?

iQ PRACTICE Go online for more practice with the vocabulary.
Practice > Unit 4 > Activities 2–3

C. PREVIEW The Web posts below and on page 60 are about fun things to do without much money. Look quickly at the Web posts. Write three things the people like to do.

1. _____

2. _____

3. _____

D. QUICK WRITE Think about fun things to do in your area. Answer these questions. Use this section for your Unit Assignment.

1. If you have money, what is a fun weekend activity?

_____

2. If you don't want to spend money, what is a fun activity?

_____

WORK WITH THE READING

 A. INVESTIGATE Read the Web posts. Find information about how to have fun without much money.

No Money?
Have Fun Anyway!

James New York Posted: 3 days ago	**Question:** How do you have fun without much money? Hi, everyone. I want to have fun, but I don't have much money. I need **ideas**. What can you do for free?
Anna Miami Posted: 3 days ago	**Re:** How do you have fun without much money? James, why don't you go to your school's sports events? I go to games every weekend. I watch soccer, basketball, baseball games, everything! It's fun to be with friends. And it's free!
Razi Dubai Posted: 2 days ago	**Re:** How do you have fun without much money? I go window-shopping with my friends! We go to expensive stores, but we only look—we don't **spend** money. So it doesn't **cost** anything.

Isabel Santiago Posted: 12 hours ago	Re: How do you have fun without much money? Our family likes going to the park. We take walks and enjoy **nature** there. Sometimes we have coffee and watch people. We try to **guess** their names and jobs. Try it!
Carlos San Salvador Posted: 4 hours ago	Re: How do you have fun without much money? **Invite** some friends to your house and cook together! My friends and I cook together once a month. First, we decide on a meal. Then we shop for the food and prepare the dishes. We usually cook food from a different country. My favorite was from Brazil. It's fun to eat with friends as well as try new recipes.
Khalid Cairo Posted: 2 hours ago	Re: How do you have fun without much money? I like to just stay home and watch TV. There are lots of good **programs**, and it's free. That's the best way to have fun.
Rob London Posted: 2 hours ago	Re: How do you have fun without much money? **Sightseeing** is fun, and you don't have to be a tourist. You can take a vacation in your own city. Walk around and enjoy the famous places.
James New York Posted: 1 hour ago	Re: How do you have fun without much money? Thanks, everyone, for all of your ideas. I'll try some of them!

ACADEMIC LANGUAGE

The phrase *as well as* is common in academic writing. It is used to add a point.

OPAL
Oxford Phrasal Academic Lexicon

B. IDENTIFY Match the person with the activity.

Sightseeing

f 1. Anna   a. go sightseeing

c 2. Razi   b. watch TV

e 3. Isabel   c. go window-shopping

d 4. Carlos   d. cook with friends

b 5. Khalid   e. watch people in the park

a 6. Rob   f. watch sports

Classifying

We often **classify** ideas or information. When we classify, we put things into groups. We put similar things together. Classifying is a good critical thinking strategy to use after you read something. It helps you understand and remember the information.

For example, perhaps you read an article about different types of vacations. You could classify the vacations into ones that are expensive and ones that are not expensive.

Expensive	Not expensive
A week in Antarctica	A week camping in a national park
A week in New York City	A week staying with relatives

A week in Antarctica is expensive.

A week camping in a national park isn't expensive.

iQ PRACTICE Go online to watch the Critical Thinking Video and check your comprehension. *Practice > Unit 4 > Activity 4*

C. **CATEGORIZE** Think about how you can classify the activities in the Web posts. One group can be "Fun activities at home." Fill in a name for another group. Then complete the chart with information from the reading. List the activities.

Fun activities at home	

D. **IDENTIFY** Answer the questions. Use information from the reading. Write complete sentences.

1. Why is it fun to watch school sports events? _____

   _____

2. What are three things to do in the park? _____

   _____

3. Which activity costs some money? _____

_____

4. Where can you go sightseeing? What are two things to do? _____

_____

E. IDENTIFY Circle the main idea for each of the posts in the reading.

1. Anna

   a. Every school has sports events.

   b. School sports events are fun and free.

   c. You can watch your favorite sports at school events.

2. Razi

   a. Window-shopping is fun, and you don't have to buy anything.

   b. Shopping with friends is fun.

   c. Window shopping at expensive stores is fun.

3. Isabel

   a. We like to go to the park and watch people there.

   b. We like to enjoy nature, and it is free.

   c. We like people watching.

4. Carlos

   a. Invite some friends to your house.

   b. Try different foods from different countries.

   c. Plan and cook a meal together with friends.

5. Khalid

   a. I like to watch TV at home.

   b. I like to stay home.

   c. Programs and movies on TV are free.

6. Rob

   a. Take a vacation and relax at home.

   b. Go sightseeing in another city.

   c. Go sightseeing in your own city.

iQ PRACTICE Go online for additional reading and comprehension.
Practice > Unit 4 > Activity 5

Collocations are words that we often use together. For example, we use the verb *play* with the noun *soccer*.

⌐ I **play soccer.**

We don't use the verbs *do* or *go* with *soccer*.

⌐ ✗ Incorrect: I **do soccer.**
└ ✗ Incorrect: I **go soccer.**

Other collocations:

⌐ give someone a ride   have an idea
└ take a trip   make friends

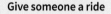

Give someone a ride

A. IDENTIFY In each collocation, circle the verb. Underline the noun.

1. Lisa and Nora **are having coffee** together.

2. Let's **make plans** for Saturday night.

3. I **have an idea**! Let's go to the beach.

4. Toshi **has fun** learning Spanish.

5. Mary **takes a walk** every day.

6. He **makes friends** with new people easily.

7. Are you hungry? **Have a snack.**

8. Can you **give** me **a ride** to the mall?

9. **Tell** me **a joke.** I need to hear something funny.

10. I am tired. I **am taking a vacation**!

B. COMPOSE Write a sentence using each collocation.

1. (make plans) _____

2. (have an idea) _____

3. (have fun) _____

4. (take a walk) _____

5. (have coffee) _____

6. (make friends) _____

7. (have a snack) _____

8. (take a vacation) _____

9. (tell someone a joke) _____

iQ PRACTICE Go online for more practice with using verb + noun collocations.
Practice > Unit 4 > Activity 6

READING SKILL Underlining and highlighting

Highlighting

When you read a text, <u>underline</u> or **highlight** the important information. This helps you remember it. Do not mark every word on the page. Mark *only* the important information.

Highlight or underline

• the main idea or topic of a paragraph;

• information such as names, dates, or times.

A. INVESTIGATE Read the newspaper article. Underline or highlight the important information.

Coming Events

1   **Storytelling.** Come listen to Jim Maddox and Mary Weston tell stories for a winter night on Wednesday, December 21, at 7 p.m. at the Davidson Library. Jim and Mary are well-known storytellers. Their stories are all about fun in the winter. Jim and Mary will also show their many photos of birds and animals. Come and enjoy a wonderful evening.

2   **Video contest.** High school students: Do you want to learn to make videos? We can teach you. The best video will win a prize of $250. We will also show the best three videos on our local TV station. For more information, meet at Town Hall at 2 p.m. on Thursday, December 22. You can borrow a camera from the library. Come learn, and improve your videos!

B. IDENTIFY Answer the questions.

1. What is the date of the storytelling event? _____

2. Where will the storytelling event take place? _____

3. How much money is the prize in the video contest? _____

4. What time is the meeting for the video contest? _____

5. Where can you borrow a camera? _____

C. IDENTIFY Look at the reading again. What fun activity does each person like? Underline or highlight the activity.

iQ PRACTICE Go online for more practice with underlining and highlighting.
Practice › Unit 4 › Activity 7

WORK WITH THE VIDEO

A. PREVIEW Are there fun, free things to do where you live? What kinds of things?

VIDEO VOCABULARY

gardening (n.) the work that you do in a garden to keep it looking attractive

route (n.) a way from one place to another

picnic (n.) a meal that you eat outside, away from home

woods (n.) a big group of trees, smaller than a forest

kids (n.) children

cheap (adj.) costing little money

iQ RESOURCES Go online to watch the video about how people have fun.
Resources › Video › Unit 4 › Unit Video

B. IDENTIFY Watch the video two or three times. Answer the questions below. There may be more than one correct answer.

1. How do James and Pete have fun when they don't have much money?

   a. having dinner with friends b. reading   c. going to the beach

2. What do Monica and Fiona do when they go on walks?

   a. listen to music   b. take a picnic   c. walk with a neighbor's dog

3. What does Marylin do if the weather is all right?

   a. go to the park   b. go to the country c. go swimming

4. What is Fiona's favorite kind of event?

   a. going to the theater   b. watching sports   c. going to weddings

5. What does Pete think you need to have fun?

   a. friends   b. money   c. free time

C. DISCUSS Discuss the questions in a group.

1. Pete likes reading and watching TV. Which do you prefer? Why?

2. Many of the people enjoy going for walks. Why do you think they like this?

3. What activities from the video are most interesting to you? Have you tried them?

WRITE WHAT YOU THINK

A. DISCUSS Discuss these questions with a partner or in a group.

1. What activities are fun for shy and quiet people?

2. What activities are fun for people who like sports?

3. What activities are fun for people who like nature?

B. SYNTHESIZE Choose and write the numbers of two questions from Activity A. Then write answers. Think about the reading and the unit video as you write. Look back at your Quick Write on page 59. Think about what you learned.

Question: ____

_____

Question: ____

_____

WRITING

OBJECTIVE ▶

At the end of this unit, you are going to write about how you have fun with your friends. Your sentences will include information from the reading, the unit video, and your own ideas.

WRITING SKILL Capitalizing proper nouns

A **noun** is a person, place, or thing. Nouns can be **proper nouns** or **common nouns**.

A proper noun is the name of a person, place, or thing. Proper nouns are always capitalized. This means some or all of the words begin with capital letters.

A common noun is a word for any person, place, or thing. Common nouns are usually only capitalized at the beginning of a sentence.

Proper Nouns		**Common Nouns**	
Maria Perez	New Zealand	woman	country
Tokyo	Spanish	city	nationality

Note: Many proper nouns have more than one word. Small words such as *the* and *of* are not usually capitalized in proper nouns.

    the Red Sea   the Gulf of Aqaba

A. IDENTIFY Read paragraph 1 of Activity A on page 64. Circle the nine proper nouns.

B. APPLY Read each pair of nouns. Which is the common noun? Which is the proper noun? Write each proper noun with a capital letter.

1. boy	william	_William_
2. smith	last name	_____
3. subaru	car company	_____
4. friday	day of the week	_____
5. hard rock cafe	restaurant	_____
6. november	month	_____
7. paris	place	_____
8. teacher	ms. andrews	_____
9. mountain	mount everest	_____

iQ PRACTICE   Go online for more practice with capitalizing proper nouns.
Practice > Unit 4 > Activity 8

- Subjects and objects can be nouns.

  - Subjects come before verbs in statements.

  - Objects come after verbs or prepositions, such as *at*, *in*, and *on*.

subject	verb	object	preposition + object
Kate	likes	the **book**.	
My **brother**	runs		in the **park**.

- **Subject pronouns** and **object pronouns** can replace nouns.

	subject pronoun	object pronoun
singular	I enjoy playing video games.	Do you want to play with me?
	You are a good cook.	Let me give you a new recipe.
	He likes making videos.	Let's give him a new video camera.
	She is a very nice person.	I like her a lot.
	Where's the ball? It's in the car.	Throw it to me!
plural	We like going to the beach.	Our friends always go with us.
	You always help our team.	We want to give you this team photo.
	They play soccer with us.	We always beat them.

- We usually use pronouns (*he/him*, *she/her*, *it/it*, *we/us*, *they/them*) after we've introduced the noun.

  Kate likes <u>the book</u>. **She** thinks **it** is very interesting. (Kate = **she**; the book = **it**)

- A **gerund** (verb + *-ing*) acts like a noun. The pronoun *it* replaces a gerund.

  I like **swimming**. **It** is fun.

      gerund

iQ RESOURCES   Go online to watch the Grammar Skill Video.
Resources › Video › Unit 4 › Grammar Skill Video

A. IDENTIFY Underline the pronouns. Then circle the noun that each pronoun refers to. Draw an arrow from the pronoun to the noun.

1. Sarah and Jill went to the mall. Then they went to a restaurant.
2. Matt likes to play tennis. He enjoys soccer, too.
3. Mika buys many books, but she doesn't always read them.
4. Ziyad will kick the ball, and Tomas will kick it back.
5. Hiro and Khalid like playing golf. They are pretty good, too!
6. Mary gave Emma and Tom some videos, and they gave her some books.

B. APPLY Complete the sentences. Write the correct subject pronoun or object pronoun.

1. Tom and I play tennis together. _____He_____ usually wins.
2. Anna likes to play board games. _____She_____ plays every weekend.
3. I don't like to play golf. I really hate _____it_____. (Obj.)
4. Mark made a video, and I helped _____him_____. (Obj.)
5. Carlos and Isabel came to my house. _____They_____ cooked dinner.
6. John and I are going to take a walk. Maybe you can join _____us_____.

iQ PRACTICE Go online for more practice with subject and object pronouns.
Practice > Unit 4 > Activity 9

iQ PRACTICE Go online for the Grammar Expansion: possessive adjectives.
Practice > Unit 4 > Activity 10

UNIT ASSIGNMENT

OBJECTIVE ▶

Write about how you have fun

In this assignment, you are going to write about how you have fun with your friends. Think about the Unit Question, "How do you have fun?" Use the reading, the unit video, and your work in this unit. Look at the Self-Assessment checklist on page 70.

iQ PRACTICE Go online to the Writing Tutor to read a writing model.
Practice > Unit 4 > Activity 11

A. BRAINSTORM Answer the questions in the chart. Make notes, but don't write sentences. Then share your ideas with a partner.

What do you do for fun?	Why is this fun for you?	When do you do this?
1.		
2.		
3.		

B. WRITE Answer the questions. Write complete sentences. Use your brainstorm notes to help you.

TIP FOR SUCCESS

Make your writing more interesting
by answering
Wh- questions—
Who? What? When?
Where? Why?

1. What do you do for fun?

2. Where do you do this?

3. When do you do this?

4. Who do you do this with?

5. Why is this fun for you?

iQ RESOURCES Go online to download and complete the outline for your sentences. *Resources > Writing Tools > Unit 4 > Outline*

iQ PRACTICE Go online to the Writing Tutor to write your sentences. *Practice > Unit 4 > Activity 12*

iQ RESOURCES Go online to download the peer review worksheet. *Resources > Writing Tools > Unit 4 > Peer Review Worksheet*

C. REVISE Review your sentences with a partner. Read your partner's sentences. Then use the peer review worksheet. Discuss the review with your partner.

D. EDIT AND REWRITE Complete the Self-Assessment checklist. Make final changes to your sentences. Be prepared to hand in your work or discuss it in class.

SELF-ASSESSMENT	Yes	No
Do you use verb + noun collocations correctly?	☐	☐
Do you use subject and object pronouns correctly?	☐	☐
Do you capitalize proper nouns?	☐	☐
Does every sentence include a subject and a verb?	☐	☐
Do you use vocabulary from the unit?	☐	☐
Does every sentence start with a capital letter and end with a period?	☐	☐

E. REFLECT Discuss these questions with a partner or group.

1. What is something new you learned in this unit?

2. Look back at the Unit Question—How do you have fun? Is your answer different now than when you started the unit? If yes, how is it different?

iQ PRACTICE Go to the online discussion board to discuss the questions. *Practice > Unit 4 > Activity 13*

TRACK YOUR SUCCESS

iQ PRACTICE Go online to check the words you have learned in this unit.
Practice ⟩ Unit 4 ⟩ Activity 14

Check (✓) the skills and strategies you learned. If you need more work on a skill, refer to the page(s) in parentheses.

CRITICAL THINKING ☐ I can classify information. (p. 61)

VOCABULARY ☐ I can use verb + noun collocations. (p. 63)

READING ☐ I can underline and highlight important ideas. (p. 64)

WRITING ☐ I can capitalize proper nouns correctly. (p. 67)

GRAMMAR ☐ I can use subject and object pronouns. (p. 68)

OBJECTIVE ▶ ☐ I can find information and ideas to write about how I have fun with my friends.

Architecture

UNIT QUESTION

What is your favorite building?

A. Discuss these questions with your classmates.

1. Look at the photo. Do you like these buildings? What do you think they are for?

2. Think about the building you are in right now. How would you describe it? What do you like about it?

3. Are there any buildings nearby that are beautiful? Why do you think so?

B. Listen to *The Q Classroom* online. Then answer these questions.

1. What is each student's favorite building? Why? Complete the chart.

	Favorite building	Reason
Yuna		
Marcus		
Felix		
Sophy		

2. Do you have a favorite building? Why do you like it?

iQ PRACTICE   Go to the online discussion board to discuss the Unit Question with your classmates. *Practice > Unit 5 > Activity 1*

UNIT OBJECTIVE

Read the email and the article. Find information and ideas to write about your favorite building.

READING 1

OBJECTIVE ▶

My Dorm Is Cool

You are going to read an email from a college student. Use the email to find information and ideas for your Unit Assignment.

PREVIEW THE READING

VOCABULARY SKILL REVIEW

As you learn new vocabulary, remember that collocations are words that we often use together. For example, the verb *share* is often followed by nouns such as *a room*, *notes*, or *a meal*. The verb *spend* is often followed by nouns such as *time* or *money*.

We put the spoons in the drawer.

A. VOCABULARY Here are some words from Reading 1. Read the sentences. Then circle the meaning of the underlined words.

1. The new <u>building</u> will have stores, restaurants, and apartments.

   a. a structure on a boat

   b. a structure on the ground

2. This chair is very <u>comfortable</u>. You can sit here and relax.

   a. expensive

   b. nice to sit on

3. My brother is <u>extremely</u> busy with his job.

   a. very

   b. not at all

4. I <u>share</u> a bedroom with my two brothers.

   a. to have or use something with another person

   b. to clean or tidy a room

5. Please put the knives and spoons in the <u>drawer</u>.

   a. a shelf on a wall

   b. a thing like a box that you can <u>pull</u> out

6. Hassan and his wife <u>spend time</u> with his grandparents on Sundays.

   a. to use time to do something

   b. to give money to someone or something

7. My bedroom window has a nice <u>view</u> of the park.

   a. what you can see from a place

   b. photograph

8. Norah has <u>modern</u> furniture in her home.

   a. popular and fashionable

   b. new and up-to-date

B. CREATE Answer these questions. Then share your answers with a partner.

1. Where do you like to spend time in your home?

   I like to spend time in my bedroom.

2. What is something that you share with others?

   I like to share food.

3. Do you like modern buildings? Why or why not?

   modern

4. What view do you have from your living room window?

   people house cars trees street

5. What is the most comfortable piece of furniture in your home?

   _____

iQ PRACTICE Go online for more practice with vocabulary.
Practice > Unit 5 > Activities 2–3

C. PREVIEW Quickly scan the email on page 76 and look at the photos to answer these questions.

1. What words can you use to describe the building?

   _____

2. Who is the email to? Who is it from?

   _____

3. How many paragraphs are in the email?

   _____

4. What is the email mostly about?

   _____

D. QUICK WRITE Think about your bedroom. Answer these questions. Remember to use this section for your Unit Assignment.

1. What furniture is in your bedroom? _____

   _____

2. Do you have a view from your window? What can you see? _____

   _____

3. What is your favorite thing in your bedroom? Why? _____

   _____

WORK WITH THE READING

 A. INVESTIGATE Read the email. Find information about the dormitory.

To: toshi21@univ.edu

From: sam18@univ.edu

Subject: My Dorm Is Cool

Dear Toshi,

1   How are you doing? How is your first year at Tokyo University? You are probably very busy, like me!

2   I love living here in Cambridge, Massachusetts, and going to school at MIT[1]! My classmates are from all over the world. I'm happy because the professors are fantastic. Of course, my classes are **extremely** difficult.

3   My dormitory[2] is very cool. It's a **modern building**. Of course, in Japan, many college students live at home. Or they live in small dorm rooms. But in the U.S., dorms are different. They are part of the university. Dorm rooms are big. My dorm is Simmons Hall. It is the best dorm at MIT. There are 340 students. It has a dining hall on the first floor. The food is good.

4   I live on the eighth floor. I **share** a room with another student, Rob. He is from Los Angeles. Every bedroom has many windows. Our bedroom has nine windows. It is a wall of windows! My bed is against the wall. Under my bed, there are nine **drawers**. My bookcase isn't very tall. It is in front of the windows. Next to the bookcase is my desk. From my desk, I have a **view** of the beautiful Charles River. Rob's part of the room is different. His desk is against the wall. His bed is above his desk! Next to the windows, he has a bookcase. In front of the windows, he has a **comfortable** chair and a lamp.

[1] **MIT:** short way to say the Massachusetts Institute of Technology, a famous science university in the United States

[2] **dormitory:** a building at a college or university where many students live

Simmons Hall, MIT   A dorm room in Simmons Hall

5   Our dorm is like a small city. There are many lounges in the building. In a lounge, you can watch TV, study, or have a snack. There is a large movie theater. We have fun activities there. We also have meetings there. There is a gym. It has lots of exercise equipment. Many people **spend time** in the gym. Of course, I just walk to class for exercise.

6   I really enjoy living here. My new friends in Simmons Hall like to have fun. But they study hard.

Write soon!

Sam

B. IDENTIFY Circle the main idea for each paragraph in the email.

1. Paragraph 3
   a. Sam's dorm is big and modern.
   b. Sam lives in Simmons Hall.
   c. There are 340 students.

2. Paragraph 4
   a. He shares a room with a student from Los Angeles.
   b. His part of the dorm room is different from Rob's part.
   c. He has a great view of the river.

3. Paragraph 5
   a. His dorm has lounges, a theater, and a gym.
   b. His dorm is in a large city.
   c. He can watch TV in a lounge.

C. IDENTIFY Circle the correct words to complete the statements.

1. Sam's classmates are from *Japan* / *all over the world*.

2. Sam's classes are *easy* / *hard*.

3. The dorm rooms in Simmons Hall are *small* / *large*.

4. The bedroom has many *beds* / *windows*.

5. From his room, Sam can see *downtown Boston* / *the Charles River*.

6. Rob's *bed* / *chair* is comfortable.

7. In a lounge, you can *watch TV* / *do exercise*.

8. For exercise, Sam *goes to the gym* / *walks to class*.

D. IDENTIFY Use the context to guess the meaning of the underlined words.

1. I'm happy because the professors are <u>fantastic</u>. (Paragraph 2)

   a. very difficult   b. very good

2. My dormitory is very <u>cool</u>. (Paragraph 3)

   a. cold   b. good

3. dorm (Paragraph 3)

   a. a place where students live   b. a place where students eat

4. dining hall (Paragraph 3)

   a. a place where students live   b. a place where students eat

5. against (Paragraph 4)

   a. across from   b. right next to

6. lounge (Paragraph 5)

   a. a place to relax   b. a game room

E. IDENTIFY Work with a partner. Look at the plan of Sam's dorm room. Label the plan with the letters from the box. Refer back to paragraph 4 of the reading. The first one is done for you.

a. Sam's bed	c. Sam's bookcase	e. Rob's bed and desk	g. Rob's lamp
b. Sam's drawers	d. Sam's desk	f. Rob's chair	

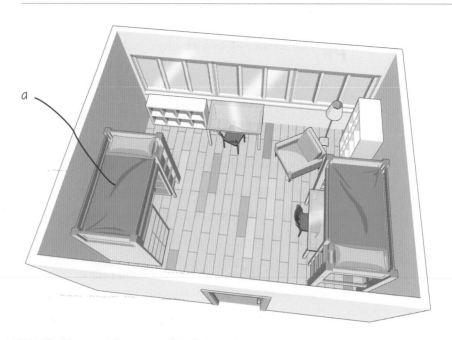

iQ PRACTICE Go online for additional reading and comprehension.
Practice › Unit 5 › Activity 4

WRITE WHAT YOU THINK

A. DISCUSS Discuss these questions in a group.

1. What do you like about your bedroom? Is it comfortable? Why or why not?

2. In your country, do university students live in dormitories? What do you know about dormitories? Are they popular? Do students prefer to live at home?

B. SYNTHESIZE Choose and write the number of one question from Activity A. Then write a response. Look back at your Quick Write on page 75. Think about what you learned.

Question: _____

My response: _____

_____

_____

_____

READING 2

A Green House

OBJECTIVE ▶

You are going to read an article about a house built by students. Use the article to find information and ideas for your Unit Assignment.

PREVIEW THE READING

A. VOCABULARY Here are some words from Reading 2. Read the definitions. Then complete the sentences on page 80.

> **bright** *(adjective)* 🗝 with a lot of light
>
> **collect** *(verb)* 🗝 to take things from different people or places and put them together
>
> **contest** *(noun)* 🗝 a game or competition that people try to win
>
> **design** *(noun)* 🗝 OPAL a drawing that shows how to make something
>
> **electricity** *(noun)* 🗝 power that comes through wires. Electricity can make heat and light and make machines work.
>
> **environment** *(noun)* 🗝 OPAL the air, water, land, animals, and plants around us
>
> **own** *(adjective)* 🗝 belonging to a particular person
>
> **space** *(noun)* 🗝 OPAL a place that is big enough for someone or something to go into or onto

🗝 Oxford 3000™ words   **OPAL** Oxford Phrasal Academic Lexicon

1. Michael's friend said he could wear her hat, but he wanted a hat of his

   _____.

2. There are too many people in this dormitory. I don't have enough

ACADEMIC LANGUAGE

The word *design* is commonly used in academic writing as both a noun and a verb. *He designs buildings. The design for the new school is amazing.*

―――――――― **OPAL**
Oxford Phrasal Academic Lexicon

   _____.

3. Don't look at the sun. It is too _____ for your eyes.

4. My friend Maria is going to _____ money to buy a present for our teacher.

5. After the big storm, many houses had no _____.

6. Before they build the bridge, there must be a good _____.

7. Mei Li was in a(n) _____. She won a lot of money.

8. Try to use less water. It is better for the _____.

iQ PRACTICE Go online for more practice with vocabulary.
Practice › Unit 5 › Activities 5–6

B. PREVIEW Look at the photos and read the captions on page 81. What is special about the house?

C. QUICK WRITE Describe what you see in one of the photos. What is in the house? Use this section for your Unit Assignment.

_____

_____

_____

_____

READING SKILL REVIEW Underlining and highlighting

Remember: you can **underline** or **highlight** important information as you read. Underline one or two important words or phrases in each paragraph. Review the Reading Skill in Unit 4, page 64.

The town of Middlebury in Vermont, USA

WORK WITH THE READING

🔊 **A. INVESTIGATE** Read the article. Find information about a house built by students.

A GREEN HOUSE

Outside view of Self-Reliance House

Inside Self-Reliance House

1   Some college students in Middlebury, Vermont, had an intelligent idea. They wanted to build a special house. They wanted the house to be modern. They also wanted the house to use a small amount of energy[1]. They decided to make a building that used the sun for heat and power. The house would be green—that is, it would be friendly to the **environment**.

2   The students worked with their professors. They created a **design**. They worked hard. They built a small house for four people. The house is about 93 square meters (1,001 sq. ft.). It is very comfortable. The kitchen, dining area, and living room are next to each other. A family can share the **space**. It is a nice place to spend time together. There are two bedrooms. One bedroom is for the parents. The children share the other bedroom.

3   The students found the materials used to build the house nearby. They did not pay for the materials to travel a long way. They put a special kind of roof on the house. The roof **collects** power from the sun, or solar energy. The power becomes **electricity**. Power from the sun also makes hot water. This means the people who live in the house have their **own** energy. They do not need to spend money for electricity or hot water.

4   The house has many windows. It is very **bright** inside. One wall is made of glass. There is a small garden inside to grow vegetables. Children in the house can watch the plants grow. They can learn about nature. The family can grow its own food.

5   The students were in a **contest** with other schools. Their school was very small and had only undergraduate[2] students. But their design was very good. Their house was better than some other houses built by students from large universities.

6   Today the house sits on the college campus. Does a family with young children live there? No. Students from the college live in the green house. The students are happy to talk to you about the design of the house. They think that everyone should save energy.

[1] **energy:** the power from electricity, gas, oil, etc., that is used to make machines work and to make heat and light
[2] **undergraduate:** studying at a college for a bachelor's degree

B. IDENTIFY What is the main purpose of the article?

☐ 1. to say where the house is now

☐ 2. to show how the students won the contest

☐ 3. to talk about the importance of plants

☐ 4. to describe a green, energy-saving house

C. IDENTIFY Put the events in the correct order. Number them 1–7.

_____ a. The children share a bedroom.

_____ b. The students decided to make a building.

_____ c. The house has many windows.

_____ d. The students created a design.

_____ e. The roof collects power from the sun.

_____ f. The students were in a contest with other schools.

_____ g. Today students live in the house.

CRITICAL THINKING STRATEGY

Restating

New ideas are sometimes hard to understand. One way to understand them better is by **restating** them. When you restate ideas, you say the same ideas again, but you use different words. When you can restate an idea, you know that you understand it well.

Original idea	Restated idea
My classes are extremely difficult.	Your courses are really hard.
Our dorm is like a small city.	There are lots of things to do in your dorm.

When learning new ideas, try to restate them. This will show that you understand the ideas.

iQ PRACTICE Go online to watch the Critical Thinking Video and check your comprehension. *Practice ⟩ Unit 5 ⟩ Activity 7*

D. APPLY Read the summary, which restates ideas from Reading 2. Complete the sentences with information from the reading.

Some college students had a(n) _____1_____. They decided

to build an unusual _____2_____. They wanted the house

to save _____3_____. So they made a house that used the

_____ for heat and power. They worked with their teachers to
4

make a(n) _____. Four _____ could live in the
5   6

house. It was a nice _____. They built the house with a special
7

_____ that took power from the sun.
8

E. RESTATE Rewrite the sentences. Keep the same meaning but use your
own words.

1. The house uses solar energy.

   The sun keeps the house warm.

2. There is a small garden to grow vegetables.

   _____

3. The students were in a competition with other students.

   _____

4. Today, students live in the house.

   _____

5. They tell other people how to save energy.

   _____

F. CATEGORIZE Complete the chart with notes from Reading 2. Then compare
your notes with a partner.

House	Notes
1. Design	
size	93 square meters
people	four
rooms	kitchen, dining area, living room, two bedrooms
2. Energy	
materials	
roof	
use of sun	
3. Other	
plants	
contest	
current location	

G. DISCUSS Discuss the questions in a group.

1. Why did the students want to use materials that were close by?

2. Why did people in the house not need to spend money for electricity?

3. The students wanted to grow vegetables in the house. Why?

4. What is most interesting to you about the green house?

5. Do you know of any green buildings near you? How do they save energy?

WORK WITH THE VIDEO

A. PREVIEW *Architecture* is the word we use to talk about the design of buildings. What famous buildings do you know about?

VIDEO VOCABULARY

canal (n.) a path that is made through the land and filled with water so that boats can travel on it

passenger (n.) a person who is traveling in a car, bus, train, or airplane but not driving or flying it

fantastic (adj.) very good; wonderful

huge (adj.) very big

NEMO Science Center

iQ RESOURCES Go online to watch the video about famous buildings in Amsterdam. *Resources ⟩ Video ⟩ Unit 5 ⟩ Unit Video*

B. IDENTIFY Watch the video two or three times. Then match the buildings in Amsterdam to their descriptions.

_____ 1. Amsterdam Centraal

_____ 2. The Rijksmuseum

_____ 3. The Muziekgebouw

_____ 4. The BIMHUIS

_____ 5. NEMO Science Center

a. a concert hall for modern music

b. great views of the city

c. a special space for jazz

d. the main railway station

e. wonderful art on the walls

C. INTERPRET Why do you think people enjoy the architecture in Amsterdam? Write your ideas.

_____

_____

WRITE WHAT YOU THINK

SYNTHESIZE Think about Reading 1, Reading 2, and the unit video as you discuss these questions. Then choose and write the number of one question. Then write a response.

1. What makes a building interesting for you?

2. Is it more important to save energy or to make a building fun to visit?

3. Describe a building that you know and tell why it is interesting.

Question: _____

My response: _____

_____

BUILDING VOCABULARY Identifying word categories

A category is a group of things. You can build your vocabulary by learning **words in a category**. For example, the category "rooms in a house" includes *living room, dining room, kitchen, bathroom,* and *bedroom.* A room in a house can also be a category. Put words for furniture and appliances under each room.

Living room	Bedroom	Kitchen
sofa lamp	bed	refrigerator

A. CATEGORIZE Make a chart like the one in the Building Vocabulary box above. Then write these words under the correct room. Some words can go in more than one room.

armchair	coffeemaker	dresser	mirror	sofa
bed	coffee table	fan	oven	stove
blender	desk	lamp	refrigerator	table
bookshelf	dishwasher	microwave	rug	toaster

B. EXTEND With a partner, add more words to your charts.

TIP FOR SUCCESS

Here are some useful adjectives to describe rooms:
large – small
sunny – dark
colorful – plain
modern – traditional

C. DISCUSS Ask and answer these questions with a partner.

1. What furniture is in your bedroom? What adjectives describe your bedroom?

2. What appliances are in your kitchen? What adjectives describe it?

3. What furniture is in your living room? What adjectives describe it?

iQ PRACTICE Go online for more practice with word categories.
Practice > Unit 5 > Activity 8

WRITING

OBJECTIVE ▶

At the end of this unit, you are going to write about your favorite building. Your sentences will include information from the readings, the unit video, and your own ideas.

GRAMMAR Prepositions of location

Prepositions of location answer the question "Where?"

The student is sitting **at** his desk.

The ruler is **in** the desk drawer.

The light is **over** / **above** the desk.

The backpack is **under** the table.

The backpack is **on** the floor.

The trash can is **next to** / **beside** the desk.

The poster is **on** the wall.

The fan is **on the right of** the desk.

The bookshelf is **behind** the fan.

The fan is **in front of** the bookshelf.

A. APPLY Look at the picture. Write sentences with prepositions of location on page 87.

1. lamp / desk _The lamp is on the desk._
2. posters / wall _The posters are on the wall._
3. bookshelf / bed _The bookshelf is under the_
4. chair / desk _The chair is in front of the desk._
5. armchair / window _The armchair is front of the window._
6. photos / bookshelf _The three photos are on the book shelf. on top of desk_

B. ANALYZE Read this paragraph about the picture in Activity A. There are five errors. Find and correct them.

I live in a very small apartment. It's crowded, but it's comfortable. My desk
is ~~beside~~ _{under} my bed. ~~In~~ _{on} my desk, I have my computer and my notebooks. To the
_{of}
^{on} left my desk, there is a small bookshelf. I have many books ~~at~~ _{in} my bookshelf.
_{next to / beside}
There is an armchair ~~over~~ my desk. I like my room, but next year I want more

space for my clothes. I need a big closet.

C. COMPOSE Look around your classroom. What do you see? Use the words to write sentences with prepositions of location.

1. teacher's desk _The teacher's desk is next to the door._
2. door _____
3. board _____
4. light _____
5. trash can _____
6. windows _____
7. computer _____
8. my desk _____

iQ PRACTICE Go online for more practice with prepositions of location.
Practice > Unit 5 > Activity 9

iQ PRACTICE Go online for the Grammar Expansion: Prepositions of time: *in, on, at. Practice > Unit 5 > Activity 10*

In the Writing Skill in Unit 3, page 49, you learned about subjects and verbs.

The **subject** and **verb** of a sentence must **agree** with each other. (A singular verb is used with a singular subject. A plural verb is used with a plural subject.)

subject verb
She **has** breakfast at the small round table.

subject verb
They **have** breakfast at the small round table.

subject verb
✓ The boys **share** an apartment.
✗ The boys **shares** an apartment.

If a sentence has more than one subject or verb, the verb(s) must still agree with the subject(s).

subject verb
My mother and father **collect** books.

subject verb
My brothers **put away** their clothes and **make** their beds.
verb

The subject and verb must agree in negative sentences.

subject verb
She **doesn't like** small rooms.

subject verb
Luis and Paul **don't like** the room.

subject verb
The room **isn't** very big.

subject verb
The rooms **aren't** very big.

The subject and verb must agree when used in questions.

verb subject
Are you at your apartment?

verb subject
Where **is** the bathroom?

verb subject verb
Does he **have** any posters in his room?

verb subject
Why **are** the closets small?

iQ RESOURCES Go online to watch the Writing Skill Video.
Resources > Video > Unit 5 > Writing Skill Video

A. APPLY Complete the statements. Use the words from the box. You may need to change the verb to make it agree with the subject.

be	describe	eat	have	share
collect	design	do	like	smell

1. We _____ dinner at 6:30.

2. Can you _____ your dorm for me? What does it look like?

3. The architects _____ small apartments.

4. I _____ to spend time in the lounge.

5. The kitchen always _____ delicious.

6. My desk _____ under the window.

7. Where _____ your family spend the most time?

8. That famous designer _____ his ideas with everyone.

9. William _____ coins from different countries.

10. Amanda and Kate _____ many books.

B. CATEGORIZE Read the sentences. Write *S* if the subject is singular. Write *P* if the subject is plural. Then circle the correct verb form.

_P_ 1. Tamara and Mina *likes* / *(like)* to relax in the dorm lounge.

____ 2. The bedroom and reading area *provides* / *provide* privacy.

____ 3. Some people *enjoy* / *enjoys* meals in the kitchen.

____ 4. Ethan *likes* / *like* reading and relaxing in his dorm room.

____ 5. Makiko's apartment *has* / *have* a nice view of the park.

____ 6. Jane's family room and living room *is* / *are* very comfortable.

____ 7. Steve *designs* / *design* and *builds* / *build* skyscrapers.

____ 8. Nabil *shares* / *share* his bedroom with his brother.

____ 9. The children *plays* / *play* computer games.

____ 10. Marie *doesn't like* / *don't like* small rooms.

C. APPLY Use *isn't/aren't or doesn't/don't* to make the sentences negative. Use a singular verb with a singular subject. Use a plural verb with a plural subject.

1. He enjoys the view. _He doesn't enjoy the view._

2. The men are in the dining room. _____

3. The apartment is very comfortable. _____

4. The bathroom has a bathtub in it. _____

5. His friends play games in the basement. _____

6. I like to walk outside. _____

D. COMPOSE Write complete sentences. For each sentence, use one phrase from Group A and one phrase from Group B. Change the verb form if necessary. There are many different ways to combine the phrases.

Group A	Group B
~~The people next door~~	have a nice apartment
My mother and father	enjoy reading
The bedroom and the reading area	like animals
Toshi	have a view of the garden
My brother	~~be very noisy~~

1. _The people next door are very noisy._

2. _____

3. _____

4. _____

5. _____

E. APPLY Use the words to make questions. Change the verb form if necessary. Then answer the questions.

1. you / live / in a small apartment _Do you live in a small apartment?_
   No, I live in a house with my family.

2. be / the walls / in your bedroom / bright _Are the walls in your bedroom bright?_
   Yes. They're bright yellow.

3. your family / play games / together _____

_____

4. you / collect / posters _____

_____

5. your friends / spend lots of time reading _____

_____

6. be / your dorm room / pretty comfortable _____

_____

iQ PRACTICE Go online for more practice with subject-verb agreement.
Practice > Unit 5 > Activity 11

UNIT ASSIGNMENT
OBJECTIVE ▶

Write about your favorite building

In this assignment, you are going to write about your favorite building. Think about the Unit Question, "What is your favorite building?" Use the readings, the unit video, and your work in this unit. Look at the Self-Assessment checklist on page 92.

iQ PRACTICE Go online to the Writing Tutor to read a writing model.
Practice > Unit 5 > Activity 12

WRITING TIP
You can use *there is* and *there are* to describe a building. The verb *be* agrees with the word after it: *There is a staircase. There are some windows on the second floor.*

A. BRAINSTORM Draw a picture of your favorite building. Write words to describe it. Then describe your building to a partner.

My favorite building is the Taj Mahal. There is a round dome on the top and towers on the sides. There is a beautiful pool in front.

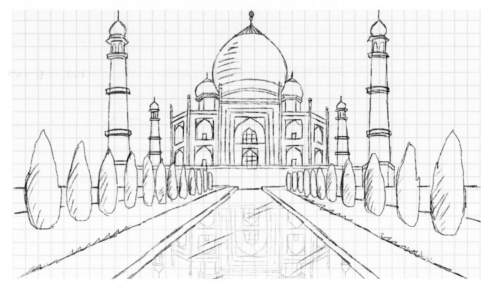

B. WRITE Answer the questions. Use complete sentences. Use your brainstorm notes to help you.

1. What is the building? Where is it located?

2. Describe the building. What does it look like?

3. Why do you like it?

iQ RESOURCES Go online to download and complete the outline for your sentences. *Resources > Writing Tools > Unit 5 > Outline*

iQ PRACTICE Go online to the Writing Tutor to write your assignment. *Practice > Unit 5 > Activity 13*

iQ RESOURCES Go online to download the peer review worksheet. *Resources > Writing Tools > Unit 5 > Peer Review Worksheet*

C. REVISE Review your sentences with a partner. Read your partner's sentences. Then use the peer review worksheet. Discuss the review with your partner.

D. EDIT AND REWRITE Complete the Self-Assessment checklist. Make final changes to your sentences. Be prepared to hand in your work or discuss it in class.

SELF-ASSESSMENT	Yes	No
Do you use prepositions of location correctly?	☐	☐
Do you use correct subject-verb agreement?	☐	☐
Do you include vocabulary from the unit?	☐	☐
Do you use capitalization and punctuation correctly?	☐	☐

E. REFLECT Discuss these questions with a partner or group.

1. What is something new you learned in this unit?

2. Look back at the Unit Question—What is your favorite building? Is your answer different now than when you started the unit? If yes, how is it different?

iQ PRACTICE Go to the online discussion board to discuss the questions. *Practice > Unit 5 > Activity 14*

TRACK YOUR SUCCESS

iQ PRACTICE Go online to check the words you have learned in this unit.
Practice > Unit 5 > Activity 15

Check (✓) the skills and strategies you learned. If you need more work on a skill, refer to the page(s) in parentheses.

READING	☐ I can underline and highlight information. (p. 80)
CRITICAL THINKING	☐ I can restate ideas in different words. (p. 82)
VOCABULARY	☐ I can identify and use categories to learn words. (p. 85)
GRAMMAR	☐ I can use prepositions of location. (p. 86)
WRITING	☐ I can use correct subject-verb agreement in different types of sentences. (p. 88)
OBJECTIVE ▶	☐ I can find information and ideas to write about my favorite building.

6 Health Sciences

READING	identifying pronoun references
VOCABULARY	using collocations
GRAMMAR	modals *can*, *could*, and *should*
CRITICAL THINKING	offering solutions
WRITING	using an editing checklist

How can you change an unhealthy habit?

A. *Habits* are regular activities. Look at the list of habits. Which habits are unhealthy? Check (✓) them. Then compare with a partner.

☐ sleep four hours every night

☐ eat fresh fruit every day

☐ drink a lot of coffee every day

☐ eat cookies and cake every day

☐ take a walk every morning

☐ drink a lot of water every day

☐ work all the time

☐ drink many sodas every day

B. Listen to *The Q Classroom* online. Then answer these questions.

1. How does each student answer the question about changing an unhealthy habit?

2. Can you think of other ways to change an unhealthy habit?

iQ PRACTICE Go to the online discussion board to discuss the Unit Question with your classmates. *Practice › Unit 6 › Activity 1*

UNIT OBJECTIVE

Read the textbook excerpt and the newspaper article. Find information and ideas to write about how to change an unhealthy habit.

READING 1

OBJECTIVE ▶

When Does a Change Become a Habit?

You are going to read a textbook excerpt about changing an unhealthy habit. Use the excerpt to find information and ideas for your Unit Assignment.

PREVIEW THE READING

A. VOCABULARY Here are some words from Reading 1. Read the definitions. Then complete the sentences.

> **become** *(verb)* 🔑 to begin to be something
>
> **behavior** *(noun)* 🔑 the way you are; the way you do and say things
>
> **expert** *(noun)* 🔑 OPAL a person who knows a lot about something
>
> **give up** *(verb phrase)* to stop doing something
>
> **goal** *(noun)* 🔑 OPAL something that you want to do very much
>
> **maybe** *(adverb)* 🔑 possibly
>
> **pay attention** *(verb phrase)* to look, listen, or think about carefully
>
> **plan** *(noun)* 🔑 something you have decided to do and how you are going to do it

🔑 Oxford 3000 keywords   **OPAL** Oxford Phrasal Academic Lexicon

1. Don't let your cough _____ a serious problem. Call your doctor today.

2. Toshi's _____ is to gain 5 pounds this month.

3. I want to _____ this diet, but my doctor says I need to lose 15 more pounds.

4. Dr. Park is a(n) _____ on food. He teaches food science at the university.

Diet

5. My friend and I are working on a(n) _____ for our science project. Then we will discuss it with our teacher.

6. Kate doesn't _____ to her health. She gets sick often.

7. The child's _____ in class is very bad. The teacher will talk with the parents about the problem.

8. I'm not sure about Friday night. _____ I will go to my friend's house.

iQ PRACTICE Go online for more practice with the vocabulary.
Practice › Unit 6 › Activities 2–3

B. PREVIEW Quickly scan the textbook excerpt below to answer these questions.

1. What kinds of habits is this excerpt about? _____

2. How many "stages of change" are there? _____

C. QUICK WRITE Think about an unhealthy habit you have. Answer these questions. Use this section for your Unit Assignment.

1. What is your unhealthy habit? _____

2. Why is it an unhealthy habit? _____

3. Why is it hard to change this habit? _____

WORK WITH THE READING

A. INVESTIGATE Read the textbook excerpt. Find information about changing unhealthy habits.

WHEN DOES A CHANGE BECOME A HABIT?

ACADEMIC LANGUAGE
The phrase *in some cases* is common in academic writing. It is used to introduce an example or a point.

OPAL
Oxford Phrasal Academic Lexicon

1   Everyone has a few unhealthy habits. For example, **maybe** you eat too much junk food[1]. Maybe you get too little sleep, or you never exercise. You know these habits aren't good for you. You should exercise more often, but you don't. Why? Because bad habits are very hard to change.

2   To change a habit, you have to change your **behavior**. It is always difficult at the beginning. But after some time, your new behavior **becomes** a new habit. In some cases, people need 20 to 70 days to change a habit. Some habits can take a year to change. According to **experts**, there are six stages of change.

3 THE SIX STAGES OF CHANGE

1. **Ignoring.** You ignore[2] the problem. You don't **pay attention** to it. You don't want to believe that it's an unhealthy habit.

2. **Thinking.** You know your habit is unhealthy, but you don't have a **plan** to change it.

[1] **junk food:** food that is quick to prepare but is bad for your health
[2] **ignore:** to know something but not do anything about it

3. **Deciding.** You decide[3] to change your bad habit. You make a plan to change. *Take action*
4. **Acting.** You start to change your unhealthy habit.
5. **Making new habits.** After many weeks, your new behavior becomes a new habit. *It's human nature*
6. **Going back to old habits.** You go back to your old habit for a day, or a week, or a month. Don't worry. This happens to everyone.

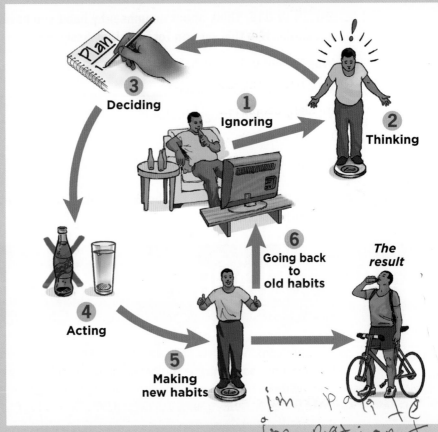

3 Deciding

1 Ignoring

2 Thinking

6 Going back to old habits

The result

4 Acting

5 Making new habits

im polite
im patient

4   People usually want to change their bad habits quickly and easily. Remember, habits take a long time to make, so they take a long time to change. Most people aren't patient. In addition, they don't want to be uncomfortable. For instance, when you start a diet, you feel hungry. If you begin an exercise program, you feel tired. You will probably be uncomfortable when you change a habit, but don't **give up**. Think about your **goal:** a healthier body. With hard work, healthy behaviors can slowly become healthy habits. *quit*

5   Changing a habit isn't easy. It takes time, and you have to be patient. But the result is a healthier and happier you.

---

[3] **decide:** to think about and choose something

B. IDENTIFY Circle the correct answers to complete the statements.

1. Most people don't change their habits because ____.

   a. it's hard to do

   b. they prefer to be unhealthy

   c. they don't know how

2. Most people need ____ to change a habit.

   a. about 20 days

   b. 20 to 70 days

   c. a year

3. ____ to their old habits.

   a. Many people return

   b. Few people return

   c. Everyone returns

4. When you first change your habit, you will probably feel ____.

   a. uncomfortable

   b. angry

   c. healthier

5. The main idea of the reading is that ____.

   a. it is too difficult to change bad habits

   b. you can change a habit if you are patient and remember your goal

   c. you will be healthier and happier if you change bad habits

C. CATEGORIZE Read the statements. Write *T* (true) or *F* (false). Write the paragraph number where you found the answer. Then correct each false statement to make it true.

_F_ 1. Most people have only one unhealthy habit. Paragraph: ____

_T_ 2. It is underlined{unhealthy} to eat junk food. Paragraph: ____

_F_ 3. Some habits take a day to change. Paragraph: ____

_F_ 4. The first stage of change is thinking about your unhealthy habit. Paragraph: ____

_T_ 5. In the acting stage, you start to change your habit. Paragraph: ____
   Action

_F_ 6. Most people are patient about changing a habit. Paragraph: ____
   impossible

Soda

D. IDENTIFY Read the sentences. What stage of change is each person at?

1. James drinks several sodas every day. He doesn't believe soda is unhealthy.

   <u>ignoring</u>

2. Matt started exercising two months ago, but he hasn't done any exercise this week.

   _____

3. Isabel eats a lot of junk food. She knows it is unhealthy, but she keeps eating it.

   _____

4. Sun-Hee wants to get more exercise. She's going to start walking to work. She wants to start an exercise class, too.

   _____

5. Mary stopped drinking coffee two months ago. Now she drinks tea every morning.

   _____

6. Carlos started a diet this week. He's eating more fruits and vegetables.

   _____

iQ PRACTICE Go online for additional reading and comprehension.
Practice > Unit 6 > Activity 4

READING SKILL **Identifying pronoun references**

Pronouns replace nouns. Writers often use a pronoun after they introduce a noun. When you read a pronoun, ask yourself, "What does this pronoun refer to?"

<u>Sarah</u> drinks a lot of <u>coffee</u>. I think **it** makes **her** very nervous.

<u>Dan's</u> goal is to lose 10 pounds. **He** says he'll reach **it** in a month.

A. IDENTIFY Read the sentences. What does the underlined pronoun refer to? Circle the words and draw an arrow.

1. (My son's behavior) is good this month. It is much better than last month.

2. You ignore the problem or don't pay attention to it.

3. You know your habit is unhealthy, but you don't have a plan to change it.

4. Running and bicycling are good ways to exercise. They are also good ways to be outside.

5. Mauro loves playing video games. He can't stop playing them.

6. Mina's grades were low last semester. Her goal is to study more this semester.

B. IDENTIFY Read the sentences from Reading 1. Underline the two pronouns. Circle the words the pronouns refer to and draw arrows.

People usually want to change their bad habits quickly and easily.

Remember, habits take a long time to make, so they take a long time to change.

Most people aren't patient. In addition, they don't want to be uncomfortable.

iQ PRACTICE Go online for more practice with identifying pronoun references. *Practice > Unit 6 > Activity 5*

WRITE WHAT YOU THINK

A. DISCUSS Discuss the questions with a partner or in a group.

1. What habit do you want to change?

2. Why is it difficult to change this habit?

3. What can you do to change this habit?

B. COMPOSE Choose and write the number of one question from Activity A. Then write a response. Look back at your Quick Write on page 97. Think about what you learned.

Question: _____

My response: _____

_____

_____

_____

READING 2

Dr. Lee on Health

You are going to read a newspaper article. A doctor answers questions from readers. Use the article to find information and ideas for your Unit Assignment.

**VOCABULARY
SKILL REVIEW**

In Unit 2, you learned about word families. What are some adjective forms of the word *stress*? Use your dictionary.

PREVIEW THE READING

A. VOCABULARY Here are some words from Reading 2. Read the sentences. Then circle the meaning of the underlined words.

1. I <u>am addicted to</u> coffee. When I don't drink coffee, I get a headache.

   a. like   b. can't stop wanting

2. I usually <u>stay up</u> until midnight on Saturday nights.

   a. do not go to bed   b. am sleepy

3. I have two tests this week. I feel a lot of <u>stress</u>.

   a. calm   b. worry

4. I want to <u>break</u> my habit of drinking sodas. They have too much sugar.

   a. start   b. stop

5. She drinks water <u>instead of</u> juice. Water is healthier.

   a. in addition to   b. in place of

6. My friend is overweight. He needs to <u>lose weight</u>.

   a. become thinner   b. become bigger

7. I want to give you some money, but <u>unfortunately</u> I don't have any.

   a. sadly   b. happily

8. I always <u>turn off</u> all of the lights in my apartment before I go out.

   a. start the electricity to b. stop the electricity to

iQ PRACTICE Go online for more practice with the vocabulary.
Practice > Unit 6 > Activities 6–7

B. PREVIEW Scan the article on page 103 for names. Complete the sentences.

1. _____ wants to lose weight.

2. _____ gives advice to readers.

3. _____ plays a lot of video games.

C. QUICK WRITE What can someone do to lose weight? Write a list of tips. Use this section for your Unit Assignment.

WORK WITH THE READING

 A. INVESTIGATE Read the article. Find information about changing unhealthy habits.

DR. LEE ON HEALTH

Sleepless Susan

1 Dear Dr. Lee,

I **am addicted to** video games. I can't stop playing them. I don't feel tired at night because I love playing games. I usually **stay up** until 3 a.m. I never get enough sleep! During the day, I am so tired. I often fall asleep in class. I feel a lot of **stress** because I don't finish my schoolwork. What's your advice[1]?

Sleepless Susan

2 Dear Susan,

Your problem isn't unusual. Many people are addicted to video games. How can you **break** this habit? First, you should make a plan. Begin to make changes slowly. For example, if you usually play games five hours a day, you could play four hours a day. Do this for the first week. The next week, you could play three hours a day. Your goal should be one hour a day of video games. Second, try a different activity. You could spend time with friends **instead of** with video games. You could **turn off** your computer at 9 p.m. and read a good book. You will want to play video games. But you need to break this habit. Good luck!

Dr. Lee

3 Dear Dr. Lee,

I love TV shows like *The Biggest Loser*. Contestants[2] on the show try to **lose weight**. Most of them are successful. They reach their goals. I want to lose 20 pounds (9 kg). Will the show's diet plan work for me?

Dan

4 Dear Dan,

The contestants on this show lose a lot of weight quickly. Experts plan everything the contestants eat and do. But what happens after the show?

5 **Unfortunately**, most contestants gain weight again. Why? After the show, contestants don't exercise five to six hours a day. They often return to unhealthy habits. If you want to lose weight, there are no quick and easy diet plans. It takes time to lose weight. You have to learn new habits. You should make your own diet plan. Remember your goal: healthier habits.

Dr. Lee

The Biggest Loser

[1] **advice:** words that you say to help someone decide what to do
[2] **contestant:** person in a contest or game show

B. IDENTIFY Circle the correct answers to complete the statements.

1. Susan is tired during the day because she ____.

   a. stays up late

   b. falls asleep in class

   c. feels a lot of stress

   d. doesn't drink coffee

2. Dr. Lee thinks that Susan should ____.

   a. get up early

   b. change her habit slowly

   c. play different games

   d. break her habit

3. Dan writes to Dr. Lee because he wants to ____.

   a. be on a TV program

   b. meet Dr. Lee

   c. lose weight

   d. gain weight

4. Dr. Lee says that Dan should ____.

   a. make his own diet plan

   b. go on the TV show

   c. lose 20 pounds

   d. not try to lose weight

C. CATEGORIZE Read the statements. Write *T* (true) or *F* (false). Write the paragraph number where you found the answer. Then correct each false statement to make it true.

____ 1. Susan usually stays up until 2 a.m. Paragraph: ____

____ 2. Dr. Lee says Susan's goal should be to play video games for 30 minutes a day. Paragraph: ____

____ 3. The contestants lose weight quickly on the show. Paragraph: ____

____ 4. After the show, most contestants continue to exercise five to six hours a day. Paragraph: ____

____ 5. Dr. Lee believes that there are no quick and easy diet plans. Paragraph: ____

____ 6. Dr. Lee gives Dan tips and suggestions for his own diet plan. Paragraph: ____

D. IDENTIFY Answer the questions. Use information from the reading.

1. Susan isn't tired at night. Why?

   _____

2. Why doesn't Susan finish her schoolwork?

   _____

3. According to Dr. Lee, does Susan have a common problem?

   _____

4. What are the two suggestions for Susan?

_____

5. How much weight does Dan want to lose?

_____

6. Why do contestants gain weight after the TV show?

_____

7. Which answer is the most helpful: Dr. Lee's reply to Susan or to Dan? Why?

_____

WORK WITH THE VIDEO

A. PREVIEW Do you think it is possible to get too much exercise? What might happen to your body?

VIDEO VOCABULARY

hormone (n.)
a substance in the body that influences growth and development

immune system (n.)
the system in your body that protects you from diseases

overdo (v.) to do too much of something

catch up (v. phr.)
to spend time doing something that you have not been able to do until now

in moderation (prep. phr.) in small quantities or amounts

iQ RESOURCES Go online to watch the video about unhealthy habits.
Resources > Video > Unit 6 > Unit Video

B. APPLY Watch the video two or three times. Complete the sentences with the words from the box.

| drink | exercise | experts | gain | healthy | hormone | sugar | weekend |

1. When you exercise, your body produces a(n) _____, cortisol.

2. Too much _____ can hurt your immune system.

3. Many people use the _____ to catch up on sleep.

4. _____ say that it is best to get the same amount of sleep every night.

5. Some people _____ weight because they eat unhealthy food when they are tired.

6. In general, fruits and vegetables are part of a(n) _____ diet.

7. A breakfast smoothie is a(n) _____ with fruits and vegetables.

8. A smoothie can contain a lot of _____.

C. **DISCUSS** Discuss the questions with a group.

1. Do you overdo anything, such as exercise, sleep, or food? Explain what you overdo (or talk about someone you know). How can you change that habit?

2. What is the most surprising thing you learned in this video?

3. Some people take vitamins to stay healthy. Do you think it is possible to take too many vitamins? Why or why not?

? WRITE WHAT YOU THINK

A. **DISCUSS** Discuss these questions with a partner or in a group. Look back at your Quick Write on page 102. Think about what you learned.

1. What unhealthy habit do you have? Why is it important to change the habit?

2. Do you have a goal? What is it?

3. Do you have a plan? What is it?

B. **SYNTHESIZE** Think about Reading 1, Reading 2, and the unit video as you discuss these questions. Then choose and write the number of one question. Then write a response.

1. In Reading 1, there are six stages of change. Think about the people in Reading 2. Which stage is Susan at? Which stage is Dan at?

2. Which habit in Reading 2 is harder to break? Why? In your opinion, how long will it take to change each habit?

Question: ____

My response: _____

_____

_____

Collocations are words that we often use together. For example, we can use the verbs *gain* or *lose* with the noun *weight*:

I **gain weight** during the holidays.   I **lose weight** during the summer.

Verb + noun collocations

break a habit   It's hard to **break the habit** of eating junk food.

set a goal   I **set a goal** to run a mile in ten minutes.

reach a goal   Next year, I will **reach my goal**. I will become a nurse.

Verb + preposition collocations

cut down on   I'm overweight. I need to **cut down on** desserts.

go off   Last weekend, I **went off** my diet. I had dessert every night.

go on   I **will go on** a new diet tomorrow.

A. APPLY Complete the sentences. Use words and collocations from the Building Vocabulary box.

1. I will _____ to graduate from a four-year college.

2. I will _____ in about five years.

3. My doctor said I should _____. I am overweight.

4. When I eat a lot of chocolate, I _____.

5. I need to _____ the _____ of sleeping in.

6. I'm going to _____ video games. I'll only play for an hour a day.

B. APPLY Answer the questions. Then ask and answer the questions with a partner.

1. What habit do you want to break? What do you want to stop doing?

_____

2. What goal do you want to reach this year?

_____

3. What goal can you set for learning vocabulary?

_____

4. What do you need to cut down on? Why?

_____

I will reach my goal.

iQ PRACTICE Go online for more practice with using collocations.
Practice > Unit 6 > Activity 8

WRITING

OBJECTIVE ▶   At the end of this unit, you are going to write about how to change an unhealthy habit. Your sentences will include information from the readings, the unit video, and your own ideas.

GRAMMAR Modals *can*, *could*, and *should*

A **modal** comes before a base form verb. Modals can be affirmative or negative.*

I **should eat** more fruit.   Sometimes I **can't sleep** at night.
─┬── ─┬─   ─┬── ─┬─
modal base verb   modal base verb

Don't put an **-s** at the end of the verb.

   ✓   Correct: He can **eat** a whole pizza.

   ✗   Incorrect: He can **eats** a whole pizza.

- Use *can / can't* to talk about possibility or ability.

   Habits **can** take years to change.   She **can't** speak Arabic.

- Use *could* to make a polite suggestion.

   You **could** come with me to my exercise class.

- Use *should / shouldn't* to give advice.

   They **should** eat more fruit.   They **shouldn't** eat junk food.

*The full forms of *shouldn't* and *can't* are *should not* and *cannot*.

iQ RESOURCES Go online to watch the Grammar Skill Video.
Resources > Video > Unit 6 > Grammar Skill Video

A. IDENTIFY Read this paragraph from Reading 2. Underline the modals *could* or *should* + verb. Label each modal as *S* (suggestion) or *A* (advice).

     Many people are addicted to video games. How can you break this habit?
A
First, you <u>should make</u> a plan. Begin to make changes slowly. For example, if you

usually play games five hours a day, you could play four hours a day. Do this for

the first week. The next week, you could play three hours a day. Your goal should

be one hour a day of video games. Second, try a different activity. You could

spend time with friends instead of with video games. You could turn off your

computer at 9:00 and read a good book. You will want to play video games. But

you need to break this habit. Good luck!

B. APPLY Complete the sentences with *can* or *can't*.

1. If I eat one potato chip, I _____can't_____ stop. I want to eat more.
2. It's difficult to break a habit, but you _____can_____ do it.
3. People _____can_____ become addicted to soda.
4. Most people _____can_____ lose weight when they exercise every day.
5. I _____can't_____ speak loudly today. I have a bad cold.

C. APPLY Complete the sentences with *should* or *shouldn't*.

1. You _____shouldn't_____ drink more than three cups of coffee a day.
2. It's very cold outside. You _____should_____ wear a jacket.
3. It's really hot. We _____shouldn't_____ go outside right now.
4. During class, you _____should_____ pay attention to the teacher.
5. David _____should_____ change his habits. He needs to eat less junk food.
6. Anna feels a lot of stress. She _____shouldn't_____ work so hard.

You shouldn't use your phone.

CRITICAL THINKING STRATEGY

Offering solutions

When you **offer solutions**, you suggest ways to solve a problem. You do not give just one solution. You offer several solutions. Offering several solutions shows that you respect the reader to make the best choice. You are not telling the reader what to do or think.

Use the modals *can* and *could* to offer possible solutions. Don't use *should* or *shouldn't*. They are stronger modals for giving advice.

To improve your grades, you **can study** with a partner.

You **could turn off** your music when you study.

You **should go** on a diet. (advice)

iQ PRACTICE Go online to watch the Critical Thinking Video and check your comprehension. *Practice > Unit 6 > Activity 9*

D. IDENTIFY Read the excerpt from Reading 2. Underline when Dr. Lee gives advice with *should*. Circle when Dr. Lee makes a suggestion with *could*.

How can you break this habit? First, you should make a plan. Begin to make changes slowly. For example, if you usually play games five hours a day, you could play four hours a day. Do this for the first week. The next week, you could play three hours a day. Your goal should be one hour a day of video games.

E. DISCUSS Read the questions. Think of two or three possible solutions for each. Use *can* and *could*. Then discuss your solutions with a partner. Which are the best solutions?

1. I stay up until 2:00 a.m. every day. I need to get more sleep. But I can't fall asleep at 11:00 p.m. What can I do?

2. I love to shop, but I spend too much money. I buy too many clothes. I want to spend less money. What can I do?

iQ PRACTICE Go online for more practice with modals *can*, *could*, and *should*. *Practice > Unit 6 > Activity 10*

iQ PRACTICE Go online for the Grammar Expansion: *Must* and *must not*. *Practice > Unit 6 > Activity 11*

WRITING SKILL Using an editing checklist

After you write, check your writing. A good way to check your writing is to use an **editing checklist**. This helps you remember common errors. When your writing has no errors, it is easy to read and understand.

Here is an editing checklist. Check your writing for each type of error.

Editing Checklist

☐	1. Capitalize the first word in a sentence or question. Capitalize proper nouns.
☐	2. Use apostrophes ('), periods (.), and question marks (?) correctly.
☐	3. Make sure every sentence has a subject and a verb. Make sure that subjects and verbs agree.
☐	4. Check that you use vocabulary correctly.
☐	5. Check words for correct spelling. Watch out for words that you often misspell.

Make your own editing checklist.

• Put a star (✱) by the type of error you make most often.

• Add words that you often misspell.

• As you learn more English, add to your checklist.

A. APPLY Read each sentence. Find and correct the capitalization error(s).

1. ~~dr. wilson~~ Dr. Wilson says ~~i~~ I should eat more fresh fruit.

2. my cousin is addicted to video games.

3. On monday, sarah is going to give up smoking.

4. i am behind in my english class.

5. richard set a goal to climb mount shasta in july.

6. the eating habits in the u.s. are very different from those in china.

7. miss garcia is an expert in asian history.

8. the hospital is on the corner of mission street and state avenue.

WRITING TIP

An apostrophe is used in contractions (*I'm*, *he's*) and to show possession (*Ahmed's*, *Ed's*). The contraction for *it is* is *it's*. The possessive for *it* is *its*. There is no apostrophe for the possessive.

B. APPLY Read each sentence. Add any missing apostrophes, periods, and question marks.

1. Could you please pay attention?

2. Marys goal is to get more sleep each night

3. Im not worried because I know losing weight will take a long time

4. Why are you so tired

5. The boys behavior shows that he has a lot of stress

6. Theyre going to create a plan for healthier meals

7. Are you addicted to your cell phone

8. Smoking is a very hard habit to break

C. APPLY Read each sentence. Correct each error with the subject or verb.

1. My grandmother is 75 years old, and she very healthy.

2. Is very careful about her diet.

3. She never eat too much food.

4. She no gain weight.

5. She and her friend goes for a walk every morning.

6. Her daily habits keeps her healthy.

D. APPLY Find and correct the ten spelling errors.

1. unhelthy
2. becoming
3. habit
4. adicted
5. stress
6. behavior
7. unfortunatly
8. diferent
9. lose weght
10. headace
11. mabe
12. expirt
13. quikly
14. atention
15. should

E. APPLY Read the student paragraph. Use the Editing Checklist to find and correct the 11 errors. How many of each type of error are there? Write the numbers in the Editing Checklist.

My older $\overset{s}{\text{S}}$ister feel a lot of stress about school. She worry$\overset{ies}{\text{about}}$ her classes $\overset{Because}{\text{she}}$ thinks her grades are bad, but they $\overset{are}{\text{very}}$ good. $\overset{M}{\text{my}}$ sister studies every nite until midnight. I think she shold relax for awhile every day. Do you think I shold tell her.

	Editing Checklist
____	1. Capitalize the first word in a sentence or question. Capitalize proper nouns.
____	2. Use apostrophes, periods, and question marks correctly.
____	3. Make sure every sentence has a subject and a verb. Make sure that subjects and verbs agree.
____	4. Check words for correct spelling.

F. IDENTIFY Look at the student's errors in the Editing Checklist in Activity E. Answer the questions.

1. What is the most common error for this student?

_____

2. What is the least common error for this student?

_____

3. What words did the student misspell?

_____

G. CREATE Look at some of your own writing. Make your own editing checklist by adding to the checklist above. Put a star (✱) next to your most common errors. Add words that you often misspell to the checklist.

iQ PRACTICE Go online for more practice with using an editing checklist. *Practice > Unit 6 > Activity 12*

UNIT ASSIGNMENT

OBJECTIVE ▶

Write about how to change an unhealthy habit

In this assignment, you are going to write about how to change an unhealthy habit. Think about the Unit Question, "How can you change an unhealthy habit?" Use the readings, the unit video, and your work in this unit. Look at the Self-Assessment checklist on page 114.

iQ PRACTICE Go online to the Writing Tutor to read a writing model.
Practice > Unit 6 > Activity 13

A. BRAINSTORM Read the text messages below. With a partner, discuss the two questions. For each question, think of several possible answers. Be sure to give advice and offer possible solutions.

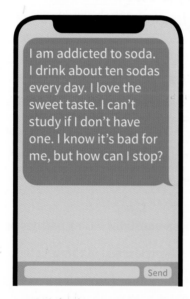

I am addicted to soda. I drink about ten sodas every day. I love the sweet taste. I can't study if I don't have one. I know it's bad for me, but how can I stop?

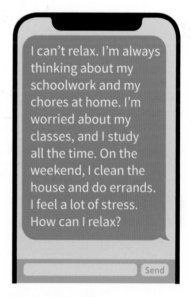

I can't relax. I'm always thinking about my schoolwork and my chores at home. I'm worried about my classes, and I study all the time. On the weekend, I clean the house and do errands. I feel a lot of stress. How can I relax?

B. WRITE Choose one question from Activity A. Answer with complete sentences. Use your brainstorm notes to help you.

iQ RESOURCES Go online to download and complete the outline for your sentences. *Resources > Writing Tools > Unit 6 > Outline*

iQ PRACTICE Go online to the Writing Tutor to write your assignment.
Practice > Unit 6 > Activity 14

iQ RESOURCES   Go online to download the peer review worksheet.
Resources > Writing Tools > Unit 6 > Peer Review Worksheet

C. REVISE Review your sentences with a partner. Read your partner's sentences. Then use the peer review worksheet. Discuss the review with your partner.

D. EDIT AND REWRITE Complete the Self-Assessment checklist. Make final changes to your sentences. Be prepared to hand in your work or discuss it in class.

SELF-ASSESSMENT	Yes	No
Do you use collocations correctly?	☐	☐
Do you use the modals *can*, *could*, and *should* correctly to give suggestions and advice?	☐	☐
Do you use vocabulary from the unit?	☐	☐
Do you capitalize the first word in each sentence?	☐	☐
Do you capitalize proper nouns?	☐	☐
Do you use apostrophes, periods, and question marks correctly?	☐	☐
Do your subjects and verbs agree?	☐	☐
Do you check your spelling?	☐	☐

E. REFLECT Discuss these questions with a partner or group.

1. What is something new you learned in this unit?

2. Look back at the Unit Question—How can you change an unhealthy habit? Is your answer different now than when you started the unit? If yes, how is it different?

iQ PRACTICE   Go to the online discussion board to discuss the questions.
Practice > Unit 6 > Activity 15

TRACK YOUR SUCCESS

iQ PRACTICE Go online to check the words and phrases you have learned in this unit. *Practice > Unit 6 > Activity 16*

Check (✓) the skills and strategies you learned. If you need more work on a skill, refer to the page(s) in parentheses.

READING	☐ I can identify pronoun references. (p. 100)
VOCABULARY	☐ I can use collocations. (p. 107)
GRAMMAR	☐ I can use modals *can*, *could*, and *should*. (p. 108)
CRITICAL THINKING	☐ I can offer solutions using *can* and *could*. (p. 109)
WRITING	☐ I can use an editing checklist. (p. 110)

OBJECTIVE ▶ ☐ I can find information and ideas to write about how to change an unhealthy habit.

Global Studies

Is it easy to live in a different country?

A. Discuss these questions with your classmates.

1. Look at the photo. Which country do you think the people are in? How do you think it is different from your country? What do you think it is like to live there?

2. Think about another country. What is different from your country? Think about the food, the traditions, and family life.

3. Do you think it is easy to live in another country? Why or why not?

B. Listen to *The Q Classroom* online. Then answer these questions.

1. How are Yuna's and Marcus's answers different?

2. Why does Sophy say that living in another country can be difficult?

3. Have you traveled to a new country? What was it like?

iQ PRACTICE Go to the online discussion board to discuss the Unit Question with your classmates. *Practice > Unit 7 > Activity 1*

UNIT OBJECTIVE ▶ Read the article and blog post. Find information and ideas to write about living in a different country or place.

READING 1

OBJECTIVE ▶

Culture Shock in the City

You are going to read an article about how moving to a new city changed a person. Find information and ideas to write about living in a different country or place for your Unit Assignment.

PREVIEW THE READING

A. VOCABULARY Here are some words from Reading 1. Read the sentences. Then write each underlined word next to the correct definition.

1. The bus was very <u>crowded</u>. I couldn't find a seat.

2. Two men robbed a bank and took a lot of money. It was a serious <u>crime</u>.

3. A man pushed past me on the sidewalk. I think he was <u>in a hurry</u>.

4. That woman is a <u>resident</u> in my apartment building.

5. Stephen's parents taught him to always say *please* and *thank you*. He is a <u>polite</u> boy.

6. After being away for ten months, Mark felt <u>homesick</u>.

7. Felix bought a table for his new <u>apartment</u>.

8. People in this small town are friendly to visitors. New people feel <u>welcome</u>.

An apartment resident

a. _____ *(noun)* a group of rooms for living in, usually on one floor of a house or big building

b. _____ *(noun)* something that someone does that is against the law

c. _____ *(adjective)* full of people

d. _____ *(adjective)* sad because you are away from home

e. _____ *(adjective)* speaking or behaving in a way that shows respect

f. _____ *(noun)* a person who lives in a place

g. _____ *(prepositional phrase)* not having enough time to do something

h. _____ *(adjective)* accepted warmly into a community

iQ PRACTICE Go online for more practice with vocabulary.
Practice ▶ Unit 7 ▶ Activities 2–3

B. PREVIEW The article below is about a woman who moves to a new city. What problems do you think she has? Check (✓) the problems.

☐ She gets lost.

☐ She misses her home.

☐ She doesn't like the food.

☐ People were not polite.

☐ She didn't feel safe.

☐ She didn't want to leave her apartment.

C. QUICK WRITE Think about a city or country you know. Answer these questions. Write for five minutes. Use this section for your Unit Assignment.

1. What is the city or country? Where is it? _____

2. What do you like about the city or country? _____

3. What do you like to do there? _____

WORK WITH THE READING

 A. INVESTIGATE Read the article. Find information about one person's experience living in a different country.

CULTURE SHOCK IN THE CITY

1   Life is different in a big city or a new country. At first, everything is exciting. But then, you may have some problems. That is what happened to Asako.

2   Asako moved from Japan to Vancouver, a big city on the west coast of Canada. At first, she was very excited. Everything was new and interesting. She enjoyed living in Vancouver. Life in the city was different. Asako thought it was fun.

3   Vancouver had good public transportation[1]. She took a bus to school. Everything happened quickly in the city. Even the people walked very fast.

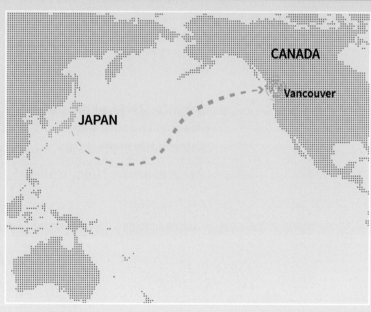

From Japan to Canada

[1]**public transportation:** buses and trains that everyone can use

4   A few months passed. Asako missed her friends and family in Japan. She felt the other **residents** of the city were not **polite**. She missed her house and Japanese food. She did not want to leave her **apartment**. She felt sad. Everything in Canada was different. She wanted to go home to Japan.

Vancouver

5   At that time, Asako saw many problems in Vancouver. The city was **crowded**. There were too many people. Everyone was always **in a hurry**. Food and rent were very expensive. And there was **crime**. She didn't always feel safe. She didn't always feel **welcome.**

6   Asako had a common problem. It is called culture shock. Most people get culture shock in a new country or city. First, they are happy. Everything is new. But then, they miss their old lives. The new country seems strange. They become **homesick**. They want to go home. They think the new country is not so good. Culture shock is almost like a sickness.

Culture shock can make you sad.

7   But Asako was smart. She knew about culture shock. She was unhappy. But she did not stay at home. She went out to try to have fun. She worked hard to make new friends. She learned about the new country. Culture shock may last for a few weeks. But it doesn't last forever.

New friends are helpful.

B. CATEGORIZE Read the statements. Write *T* (true) or *F* (false.) Write the paragraph number where you found the answer. Then correct each false statement to make it true.

_____ 1. Asako moved from Japan to Montreal. Paragraph: _____

_____

_____ 2. At first, she thought that life in the city was fun. Paragraph: _____

_____

_____ 3. People in Vancouver move very slowly. Paragraph: _____

_____

_____ 4. Asako missed her family. Paragraph: _____

_____

_____ 5. She enjoyed going out and doing things. Paragraph: _____

_____

_____ 6. The city had many people in it. Paragraph: _____

_____

_____ 7. People with culture shock miss their old life at home. Paragraph: _____

_____

_____ 8. Culture shock lasts forever. Paragraph: _____

_____

C. IDENTIFY Put the events in the correct order. Number them 1–6.

_____ a. Asako went out to try and have fun.

_____ b. She missed her friends and family in Japan.

_____ c. Later, she began to enjoy life in Vancouver.

_____ d. Asako moved to Vancouver.

_____ e. She saw many problems in Vancouver.

_____ f. At first, Asako enjoyed living in a big city.

D. INTERPRET Circle the correct words to complete the statements.

1. When Asako first moved to Canada she was _____.

   a. afraid   b. excited   c. bored

2. One good thing about Vancouver is its _____.

   a. beautiful parks   b. friendly people   c. public transportation

3. People in Vancouver walk _____.

   a. quickly   b. slowly   c. often

4. When there are too many people, you can feel _____.

   a. afraid   b. alone   c. crowded

5. Asako didn't feel safe because of the _____.

   a. crime   b. people   c. residents

E. EXPLAIN Answer the questions. Use information from Reading 1.

1. What did Asako like about Canada at first?

_____

2. What is culture shock like? How do people feel if they get it?

_____

3. How can you feel better if you get culture shock?

_____

F. EXTEND Answer the questions. Think about your own experience.

1. How might you feel after traveling to a new country?

   _____

2. What is the most surprising or interesting idea in the reading? Why?

   _____

iQ PRACTICE Go online for additional reading and comprehension.
Practice > Unit 7 > Activity 4

? WRITE WHAT YOU THINK

A. DISCUSS Discuss these questions in a group.

1. Give an example of a time when you were in a different country or city. Describe how you felt during and after that time.

2. Do you think it is important for people to travel to different places? Why? How can it be useful?

B. SYNTHESIZE Choose and write the number of one question from Activity A. Then write a response. Look back at your Quick Write on page 119. Think about what you learned.

Question: _____

My response: _____

_____

_____

READING SKILL Building reading fluency

Reading fluency means how quickly and easily you read. It is important to increase your reading speed. Here are two ways to build your reading fluency.

- Move your eyes across each line and down the article. Keep your eyes moving. Don't stop for words you don't know.

- The first time you read, look for the main ideas.

- The second time, pay attention to details and vocabulary.

Sometimes you need to read an article three or four times. Each time, try to read it more quickly. Rereading something can increase your reading fluency.

A. APPLY Do three timed readings of Reading 1. Each time, read for 30 seconds. Follow these steps.

1. When your teacher says "Start," read from the beginning of Reading 1.

2. When your teacher says "Stop," write a small *1* exactly where you stop.

3. Do the timed reading two more times. Each time, start at the beginning. The second time, write a *2* where you stop. The third time, write a *3*.

4. Did you read more each time? Did you increase your reading fluency?

TIP FOR SUCCESS

Remember, you don't have to understand every word the first time you read an article. Even with some words missing in Activity B, you can understand the paragraph's main idea.

B. APPLY Nine words are missing from this paragraph, but you don't need them to understand the main ideas. Read the paragraph without stopping. Then circle the correct answers below.

Residents of a city are interested in the   of life in a city. They want to live happily and   in a city. For example, places for social activities and events, public areas and beautiful parks, and openness are all important for residents. But tourists are   in different things. Tourists want to see   things such as   museums and famous places. They want to experience the most   places in a city. Easy transportation, friendly people, and   experiences are all important to tourists. For this   , cities with the best lifestyle are not always the top tourist cities. And the top tourist   are not always the best places to live.

1. This article discusses _____.

   a. only residents   c. residents and friendly people

   b. tourists and residents   d. only tourists

2. Residents and tourists are interested in _____ things in a city.

   a. the same   c. different

   b. famous   d. fun

3. The city with the best lifestyle is _____ the top tourist city.

   a. usually   c. never

   b. always   d. not always

iQ PRACTICE Go online for more practice with building reading fluency. *Practice > Unit 7 > Activity 5*

Life in a New City

You are going to read a blog post about readers' first impressions of Berlin, Germany. Use the blog post to find information and ideas for your Unit Assignment.

PREVIEW THE READING

VOCABULARY SKILL REVIEW

In Unit 6, you learned that collocations are words that we often use together. What are some collocations with the words *international*, *impression*, and *opinion*?

A. VOCABULARY Here are some words from Reading 2. Read the sentences. Then circle the correct meaning of the underlined words.

1. I heard a <u>complaint</u> about this restaurant. The food is not very good.

   a. a comment from an unhappy person   b. a comment from a happy person

2. In my <u>opinion</u>, the city lifestyle is wonderful and exciting.

   a. a thought about something   b. a report about a topic

3. There are many <u>international</u> students at this university.

   a. from different countries   b. intelligent

4. Pat's friendliness is her best <u>characteristic</u>.

   a. special thing about her   b. unusual idea about her

5. The air in the city is dirty and polluted. It needs to <u>improve</u>.

   a. get worse   b. get better

6. My first <u>impression</u> of the neighborhood was good. I liked it because there were many beautiful trees.

   a. idea or feeling   b. town or city

7. On weekends, I buy fresh fruit at a farmers' <u>market</u> downtown. Each farmer sells a good variety of fruits.

   a. place to eat food   b. place to shop for things

8. This museum is very expensive. I'm <u>surprised</u>. I thought it was free.

   a. feeling serious about something   b. feeling caught off guard by something unexpected

iQ PRACTICE   Go online for more practice with the vocabulary.
Practice ▸ Unit 7 ▸ Activities 6–7

B. PREVIEW With a partner, talk about Berlin, Germany. Together, make a list of everything you know about Berlin.

C. QUICK WRITE Why do you think some people may enjoy living in Berlin? Write a list. Use this section for your Unit Assignment.

_____

_____

WORK WITH THE READING

A. INVESTIGATE Read the blog post. Find information about why people live in cities.

Home	🔍 Sign in 👤

ABOUT   LATEST POSTS   ARCHIVES   SUBSCRIBE

LIFE IN A NEW CITY

1   Some long-time residents of Berlin have **complaints** about their city. Last week, we invited some of our newer residents to give their **opinions**.

Mei

2   I am from Taiwan, and I moved here two years ago. I'm studying engineering at Humboldt University. Berlin is very **international**. That is its best **characteristic**. There are students and professors from all over the world. But my first **impression** was not very good. During my first year here, many students didn't seem friendly. I was shy because my German wasn't very good. When my German **improved**, I tried to talk to other students more. After several months, I made a few good friends. I started to enjoy living in the city. Now I have a good opinion of Berlin, and I enjoy studying here.

ACADEMIC LANGUAGE

In academic writing, *characteristic* is more common as a noun than an adjective.

⌐ **OPAL**

Oxford Phrasal Academic Lexicon

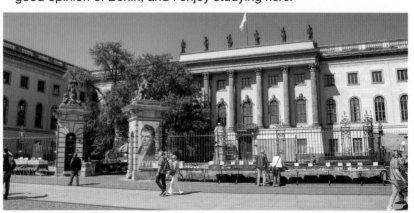

Humboldt University

Tala

3   I am from the Philippines, and I moved here with my family five years ago. I don't like cold weather, so at first, I was unhappy. But people here don't stay inside in the winter. For example, last December, I visited the outdoor **markets** with my parents. It was cold, and it was dark at 3:30 p.m. But the markets were very colorful! My family and I walked around for hours. We went to many stores. We enjoyed the beautiful lights. Everyone was outside, having fun! When we became cold, we had a hot drink at a cafe. Later in the evening, there was a free event. On that winter night, the city was exciting. The next day, I went ice skating with my friends. There was a beautiful view of the city from the skating rink. Now I think differently about the cold winter months.

An outdoor Christmas market in Berlin, Germany

Pedro

4   My first impression of Berlin was very good. This city really welcomes bicyclists, and that is very unusual. I love biking, but it can be dangerous in a city. On my first weekend in Berlin, I biked all over the city. There are special red bike paths everywhere, and they are very safe. I was really **surprised**. Also, I explored the beautiful city parks and gardens.

Red bike paths in Berlin

B. CATEGORIZE Read the statements. Write *T* (true) or *F* (false). Write the number of the paragraph where you found the answer. Then correct each false statement to make it true.

1. Mei moved to Berlin five years ago. Paragraph: _T_

   _____

2. Mei didn't speak German very well when she arrived. Paragraph: _T_

   _____

3. Mei doesn't like studying in Berlin now. Paragraph: _F_

   _____

4. Residents of Berlin enjoy spending time outside in the winter. Paragraph: _T_

   _____

5. Tala didn't like the outdoor markets. Paragraph: _F_

   _____

6. Tala enjoyed skiing in Berlin. Paragraph: F

_____

7. Pedro enjoys running in the city parks in Berlin. Paragraph: F

_____

8. The bike paths in Berlin are red. Paragraph: I

_____

C. **CATEGORIZE** Fill in the chart. How does each person's impression of Berlin change? Then answer the questions below.

	First impression	Later impression
Mei	Students weren't friendly.	
Tala	She didn't like the cold weather.	
Pedro		He still feels the same.

1. Which person had a very good first impression? Why?

_____

2. For the other two people, what happened to change their impressions?

_____

D. **EXPLAIN** Answer the questions.

1. What did you learn about Berlin? Write three things.

_____

_____

_____

2. At first, Mei's impression of Berlin was not very good. Why?

_____

3. Would you enjoy visiting the outdoor markets in winter? Why or why not?

_____

4. How is Berlin similar to your city?

_____

5. How is Berlin different from your city?

_____

CRITICAL THINKING STRATEGY

Separating fact and opinion

Some statements are **facts**. A fact is something that you know is true.

⌈ Berlin is in Germany. In Berlin, there are many bicycle paths.

Most people agree that this is true. We can check, measure, or look up facts.

Other statements are **opinions.** An opinion is what you think about someone or something. Another person may disagree.

⌈ Berlin is a beautiful city.
⌊ Shopping in markets is fun.

Maybe you think that shopping in markets is fun. Another person might not think so.

It is useful to be able to separate facts from opinions.

iQ PRACTICE Go online to watch the Critical Thinking Video and check your comprehension. *Practice > Unit 7 > Activity 8*

E. IDENTIFY Are the statements fact or opinion? Write *F* (fact) or *O* (opinion).

____ 1. Markets in Berlin are open in the evening.

____ 2. Students at this school are not friendly.

____ 3. In winter, it gets dark at 3:30 p.m.

____ 4. Berlin is an exciting city.

____ 5. About 4 million people live in Berlin.

____ 6. Biking in Berlin is fun.

WORK WITH THE VIDEO

A. PREVIEW Most of us live in one place. Do you know of any groups of people who travel from one place to another?

VIDEO VOCABULARY

photographer (n.)
a person who takes photographs, especially as a job

journey (n.)
a long trip from one place to another

head off (v.)
to leave, especially in a certain direction

incredible (adj.)
impossible or very difficult to believe

temperature (n.)
how hot or cold a thing or place is

grass (n.) a plant with thin green leaves that covers fields and yards. Cows and sheep eat grass.

iQ RESOURCES Go online to watch the video about an unusual journey.
Resources > Video > Unit 7 > Unit Video

B. IDENTIFY Watch the video two or three times. Then read the statements. Write *T* (True) or *F* (False).

_____ 1. The family is traveling from their summer home to their winter home.

_____ 2. The tents they sleep in are made by the travelers.

_____ 3. Tim's group stays behind to cook.

_____ 4. The temperature is cold on the trip.

_____ 5. They travel on the journey so the animals get exercise.

C. DISCUSS Discuss the questions in a group.

1. Have you ever been on a long trip? Where did you go?

2. What do you think are the good things about going on long trips?

3. What do you think is difficult about traveling for a long time?

WRITE WHAT YOU THINK

A. EXTEND Imagine that Mei, Tala, and Pedro are coming to your city or town. Complete the chart. Then discuss your answers with a partner.

Mei should see . . . because . . .   *I can take her to . . .*

	Where should you take this visitor?	What can you show your visitor? Why?
Mei		
Tala		
Pedro		

B. DISCUSS Discuss the questions with a partner or in a group. Look back at your Quick Write on page 125. Think about what you learned.

1. Why do people like to live in Berlin?

2. What would you enjoy in Berlin? Why?

C. SYNTHESIZE Think about Reading 1, Reading 2, and the unit video as you discuss these questions. Then choose and write the number of one question. Then write a response.

1. Think about the experiences of the students in Readings 1 and 2. Which student is most like you? Why?

2. In your opinion, is it easy to live in a different city? Give examples.

Question: _____

My response: _____

_____

BUILDING VOCABULARY Identifying word families

Pollution

When you learn a new word, use your dictionary to learn other words in the same **word family**. For example, look up *pollution* in your dictionary. You will find the verb *pollute* above it. To review word families, see Unit 2, page 25.

---

pol·lute /pəˈlut/ *verb* (**pol·lutes, pol·lut·ing, pol·lut·ed**)
to make the air, rivers, etc. dirty and dangerous: *Many of our rivers are polluted with chemicals from factories.*

pol·lu·tion /pəˈluʃn/ *noun* [noncount]
1 the action of making the air, rivers, etc. dirty and dangerous: *We must stop the **pollution** of our beaches.*
2 dirty and dangerous chemicals, gases, etc. that harm the environment: *Our rivers are full of pollution.*

All dictionary entries adapted from the *Oxford American Dictionary for Learners of English* © Oxford University Press 2011

A. CATEGORIZE Complete the chart. Use your dictionary. (An **X** means that a word doesn't exist or that you don't need to know it.)

	Noun	Verb	Adjective
1.		appear	X
2.			interesting; interested
3.	X		modern
4.		X	public
5.	pollution		
6.			relaxing; relaxed
7.		X	safe
8.	society		social

B. APPLY Complete the sentences. Use the correct noun, verb, or adjective from Activity A. More than one answer may be correct.

1. I like to _____ relax _____ in the park. It is a(n) _____ place.

2. Cars _____ the air and make it dirty. Cars cause

   _____ in the city.

3. I live in a very _____ neighborhood. I don't worry about my

   _____.

4. Our airport is very old. Next year, the city will _____ it with

   free Wi-Fi, new furniture, and new stores.

5. I'm a very talkative and _____ person. I like to

   _____ with my friends in the cafeteria after class.

6. The post office and the library are _____ buildings. Those

   buildings are open to the _____ six days a week.

iQ PRACTICE Go online for more practice with identifying word families.
Practice > Unit 7 > Activity 9

A library in Pärnu, Estonia

WRITING

OBJECTIVE ▶   At the end of this unit, you are going to write about your experience of a different country or place. Your sentences will include information from the readings, the unit video, and your own ideas.

GRAMMAR Past of *be*; Simple past affirmative statements

Past of *be*

Use the **past of *be*** to identify and describe people, places, and things in the past.

Affirmative and negative statements

subject	*be*	(*not*)	
I	**was**		happy in Hong Kong.
You We They	**were**	**(not)**	at the outdoor market.
He She It	**was**		in the public garden.

You can contract *be* + *not* in negative statements:

was not = wasn't   were not = weren't

To ask *yes/no* questions, use a past form of *be*. To ask information questions, use a *wh-* word + past form of *be*.

Yes/No questions

be	subject	
Was	the apartment	expensive?
Were	the streets	safe?

Short answers

yes	*no*
Yes, it **was**.	No, it **wasn't**.
Yes, they **were**.	No, they **weren't**.

Information questions

wh- word	*be*	subject	
Who	**was**	the writer?	
What	**were**	the questions	about?
Where	**was**	the museum?	

Answers

Charles Dickens **was** the writer.

They **were** about cities.

It **was** near the park.

Simple past affirmative statements

The **simple past** describes completed actions in the past.

The **simple past** verb form is the same for all subjects.

> Last summer, we **visited** Miami.
>
> My cousins **welcomed** us into their home.
>
> The train **stopped** at the station.
>
> Ana **stayed** home and **studied** for the test.

Spelling of simple past verbs

Add -*ed* after most verbs. Add -*d* after verbs that end in -*e*.	trave**led**, walk**ed** welcom**ed**, improv**ed**
If a one-syllable verb ends in a vowel + consonant, double the consonant and add -*ed*.	plan**ned**, stop**ped**
If the verb ends in a consonant + -*y*, change the *y* to *i* and add -*ed*.	stud**ied**, tr**ied**
If the verb ends in a vowel + -*y*, add -*ed*.	play**ed**, stay**ed**

iQ RESOURCES Go online to watch the Grammar Skill Video.
Resources > Video > Unit 7 > Grammar Skill Video

A. APPLY Complete each sentence with *was, were, wasn't,* or *weren't.*

1. The city _____ very clean. There _____ any trash in the streets.

2. The sky _____ clear and blue. The air _____ polluted.

3. The taxi _____ very expensive. Next time, I will take a bus.

4. The residents _____ worried about crime. The city was very safe.

5. We _____ tired after the trip. The roads _____ very crowded, and traffic moved slowly.

6. Last year, the economy in my area _____ very bad.

7. I _____ happy about my new office. It was very dark.

A clear sky

B. APPLY Complete the two paragraphs about Dubai.

This paragraph is a general description of Dubai. Use the simple present.

Dubai, United Arab Emirates

Dubai in the United Arab Emirates _____ a very impressive,
                                            1. (be)

modern city. It _____ some of the tallest buildings in the
                    2. (have)

world, and the shopping malls, hotels, and restaurants _____ all
                                                              3. (be)

very new—and expensive! Dubai _____ on a peninsula, and it
                                        4. (be)

_____ beautiful beaches. The weather _____
        5. (have)   6. (be)

very sunny and warm.

This paragraph is about the writer's first impressions of Dubai. Use the simple past.

My wife and I _____ to Dubai last year. My first impression
                    7. (move)

of Dubai _____ good. The people _____ very
            8. (be)   9. (be)

welcoming and _____ our questions. On the weekend, we
                    10. (answer)

_____ down narrow streets in the old market area. However, the
        11. (walk)

daytime temperatures _____ very hot. I _____ to
                            12. (be)   13. (try)

stay inside with the air conditioning.

C. COMPOSE Put the words in the correct order to make questions. Then ask
and answer the questions with a partner.

1. hot / it / was / yesterday

   _____

2. people / were / friendly

   _____

3. school building / last night / was / the / open

   _____

4. your teacher / who / last year / was

   _____

iQ PRACTICE Go online for more practice with the past of *be* and simple past affirmative statements. *Practice ˃ Unit 7 ˃ Activity 10*

iQ PRACTICE Go online for the Grammar Expansion: Past time expressions. *Practice ˃ Unit 7 ˃ Activity 11*

WRITING SKILL Identifying fragments and complete sentences

A sentence with no subject or no verb is not complete. It is a **sentence fragment**.

- ✓ **She is** interested in history.
- ✗ Is interested in history. (no subject)

- ✓ The **residents relaxed** in the park.
- ✗ The residents in the park. (no verb)

A **complete sentence** needs a subject and a verb. The subject is who or what the sentence is about. The verb tells what the subject does or what the subject thinks, feels, or is. To review simple sentences, see Unit 1, page 13.

The city is old and beautiful.
    subject verb

The residents enjoy their city parks.
    subject   verb

Always check your writing and ask: *Does the sentence have a subject? Does the sentence have a verb?* Identify and correct any sentence fragments.

A. IDENTIFY Read the sentences about the city of Boston. Underline the subjects and circle the verbs. Some sentences may have more than one subject or more than one verb.

1. <u>My family</u> and I (went) to Boston four years ago.

2. Boston is a very historic city.

3. We visited many historic buildings in the downtown area.

4. My family and I went to the famous public gardens and walked around.

5. We saw Quincy Market and had lunch there.

6. We watched sailboats on the Charles River.

B. CATEGORIZE Read each sentence. Write *C* (complete sentence) or *F* (fragment).

____ 1. The city very modern with some fantastic skyscrapers.

____ 2. It has a strong economy and good public transportation.

____ 3. The pollution not too bad during my visit last year.

____ 4. Enjoyed going to the farmers' market.

____ 5. The city seemed very safe and relaxing.

____ 6. After lunch, went to the new art museum.

____ 7. The shopping in the city was really fantastic.

C. COMPOSE Correct the fragments in Activity B. Use a subject or a verb from the box to make complete sentences.

is	my friends and I	was	we

1. _____

2. _____

3. _____

4. _____

iQ PRACTICE Go online for more practice with identifying fragments and complete sentences. *Practice ⟩ Unit 7 ⟩ Activity 12*

Public transportation

UNIT ASSIGNMENT Write about a new place

OBJECTIVE ▶

In this assignment, you are going to write about your experience of a different country or place. Think about the Unit Question, "Is it easy to live in a different country?" Use the readings, the unit video, and your work in this unit. Look at the Self-Assessment checklist on page 138.

iQ PRACTICE Go online to the Writing Tutor to read a writing model.
Practice > Unit 7 > Activity 13

A. BRAINSTORM Think about a different city, country, or place you visited. Complete the T-chart. Then share your ideas with a partner.

Facts about the place	Your opinions about the place

B. WRITE Answer the questions. Write several sentences for each question. Use your brainstorm chart to help you.

1. When did you visit the place? Who did you go with?

2. What did you see or do?

3. What was the most interesting thing about the place?

4. Was it easy or difficult to live there? Explain your answer.

iQ RESOURCES Go online to download and complete the outline for your sentences. *Resources > Writing Tools > Unit 7 > Outline*

iQ PRACTICE Go online to the Writing Tutor to write your assignment.
Practice > Unit 7 > Activity 14

iQ RESOURCES Go online to download the peer review worksheet.
Resources > Writing Tools > Unit 7 > Peer Review Worksheet

C. REVISE Review your sentences with a partner. Read your partner's sentences. Then use the peer review worksheet. Discuss the review with your partner.

D. EDIT AND REWRITE Complete the Self-Assessment checklist. Make final changes to your sentences. Be prepared to hand in your work or discuss it in class.

SELF-ASSESSMENT	Yes	No
Does every sentence have a subject and a verb?	☐	☐
Do you write in complete sentences?	☐	☐
Do you use the correct form of vocabulary words from this unit?	☐	☐
Do you use the simple past correctly?	☐	☐

E. REFLECT Discuss these questions with a partner or group.

1. What is something new you learned in this unit?

2. Look back at the Unit Question—Is it easy to live in a different country? Is your answer different now than when you started the unit? If yes, how is it different?

iQ PRACTICE Go to the online discussion board to discuss the questions.
Practice > Unit 7 > Activity 15

TRACK YOUR SUCCESS

iQ PRACTICE Go online to check the words and phrases you have learned in this unit. *Practice > Unit 7 > Activity 16*

Check (✓) the skills you learned. If you need more work on a skill, refer to the page(s) in parentheses.

READING	☐ I can build my reading fluency. (p. 122)
CRITICAL THINKING	☐ I can separate fact and opinion. (p. 128)
VOCABULARY	☐ I can use the dictionary to identify word families. (p. 130)
GRAMMAR	☐ I can use the past of *be* and the simple past in affirmative statements. (p. 132)
WRITING	☐ I can identify fragments and write in complete sentences. (p. 135)
OBJECTIVE ▶	☐ I can find information and ideas to write about living in a different country or place.

Technology

8

How can technology help people?

A. Discuss these questions with your classmates.

1. How do you use technology? List five ways.

   I use technology to: _____ _____

   _____ _____ _____

2. How does technology help you the most?

B. Listen to *The Q Classroom* online. Then answer these questions.

1. How does each student answer the question about technology?
   Complete the chart.

	How technology helps us
Sophy	
Yuna	
Marcus	
Felix	

2. What are some other ways that technology helps people?

iQ PRACTICE Go to the online discussion board to discuss the
Unit Question with your classmates. *Practice > Unit 8 > Activity 1*

UNIT OBJECTIVE

Read the feature article and the article from a news magazine. Find information
and ideas to write about how technology can help people.

READING 1

OBJECTIVE ▶

Be My Eyes

You are going to read a feature article. The article is about a man who invented a very helpful app. Use the article to find information and ideas for your Unit Assignment.

PREVIEW THE READING

A. VOCABULARY Here are some words from Reading 1. Read the definitions. Then complete the sentences.

> **daily** *(adjective)* 🔑 happening every day
>
> **explain** *(verb)* 🔑 OPAL to tell someone about something so they understand it
>
> **independent** *(adjective)* 🔑 OPAL not needing or wanting help
>
> **introduce** *(verb)* 🔑 OPAL to bring in something new
>
> **quickly** *(adverb)* 🔑 fast; in a short time
>
> **simple** *(adjective)* 🔑 OPAL easy to do or understand
>
> **solution** *(noun)* 🔑 OPAL the answer to a problem
>
> **volunteer** *(noun)* 🔑 a person who does a job without being paid

🔑 Oxford 3000™ words   **OPAL** Oxford Phrasal Academic Lexicon

1. Doctors say you should do _____ exercises.

2. It's hard to find the _____ to this math problem.

3. We need to walk _____. The bus will be here soon.

4. Use a topic sentence to _____ the main idea of your paragraph.

5. To learn how to cook, start with _____ recipes.

6. Young children want to be _____. They like to do things themselves.

7. Some parents _____ at their children's school. They help teachers and do special projects.

8. Will you please _____ our biology assignment to me? I don't understand it.

iQ PRACTICE Go online for more practice with vocabulary.
Practice › Unit 8 › Activities 2–3

B. PREVIEW Look at the photos and read the caption and quotation on page 144. Then answer the question.

What do you think Hans Jørgen Wiberg did? Check (✓) your answer.

☐ a. He was a volunteer.

☐ b. He introduced an app to help people.

☐ c. He taught people how to cook.

C. QUICK WRITE Answer these questions. Use this section for your Unit Assignment.

1. How can technology help students? _____

_____

2. How can technology help doctors? _____

_____

3. How can technology help a blind person, someone who cannot see? _____

_____

READING SKILL REVIEW Building reading fluency

Remember: you can increase your **reading fluency** (speed and understanding) with practice. Read an article several times. The first time, read for the main idea. The second time, read for details. The third time, increase your reading fluency. Don't stop for new words. Review the Reading Skill in Unit 7, page 122.

WORK WITH THE READING

 A. INVESTIGATE Read the article three times. Find information about how technology can help people. Read the first time for the main idea. Then read again for details. Finally, read a third time for fluency. Don't stop for new words.

Be My Eyes

1   Imagine that you are blind. You can't see anything. You are in your kitchen, and you are making dinner. You need a can of tomatoes. You have three cans, but you don't know which one has tomatoes. What do you do? As a blind person, this is just one example of a **daily** problem. A sighted person[1] could quickly identify the can of tomatoes.

2   Hans Jørgen Wiberg is a Danish furniture-maker. He had these problems every day. He has very low vision. In his free time, he taught blind and low-vision people[2] how to cook. They wanted to be **independent**. He understood their difficulties. Sometimes they just needed one piece of information. Usually, a blind person has to ask someone for help. But blind people want to do things for themselves. It is difficult to always ask someone for help.

Hans Jørgen Wiberg

3   Wiberg thought of an easy **solution** to this problem. He could design a cell phone app. A blind person can use the app to make a video call to a sighted **volunteer**. The volunteer can answer the question by looking at the video on a cell phone. The blind person can **quickly** get the information. After he had this idea, Wiberg wanted to design his app.

4   In 2012, Wiberg met Christian Erfurt, a young business student. Wiberg **explained** his idea. Erfurt was very excited to work with Wiberg. Three years later, they **introduced** their app. It is called Be My Eyes. After 24 hours, there were 1,100 blind and low-vision users. There were over 10,000 volunteers. In 2017, they introduced a new app. Now the average reply to a call is in 20 seconds. The usual call finishes in less than two minutes. It is quick for the caller and the volunteer.

5   The app is very popular. There are over 100,000 blind and low-vision users and 1.7 million volunteers. Users are in more than 150 countries around the world. This **simple** app is changing the lives of many people, including the volunteers.

> "It's my hope that by helping each other as an online community, Be My Eyes will make a big difference in the everyday lives of blind people all over the world."
>
> – Hans Jørgen Wiberg, founder of Be My Eyes

[1] **sighted person:** someone who is able to see
[2] **low-vision people:** people who can't see well

B. IDENTIFY Answer the questions. Use information from Reading 1.

1. What kind of daily activity is difficult for a blind person?

    _____

2. What was Wiberg's solution to this problem?

    _____

3. When did Wiberg meet Erfurt?

    _____

4. What is the name of the app they designed?

    _____

5. Did the app become popular quickly?

    _____

6. When did Wiberg introduce a new app?

    _____

C. CATEGORIZE Read the statements. Write *T* (true) or *F* (false). Write the paragraph number where you found the answer. Then correct the false statements.

____ 1. A sighted person is not blind. Paragraph: ____

        _____

____ 2. Hans Jørgen Wiberg makes clothing. Paragraph: ____

        _____

____ 3. Wiberg and Christian Erfurt first introduced their app in 2012.
         Paragraph: ____

        _____

____ 4. A volunteer usually answers a call within 20 seconds. Paragraph: ____

        _____

____ 5. There are over 2 million volunteers. Paragraph: ____

        _____

____ 6. Be My Eyes users are in over 150 countries. Paragraph: ____

        _____

CRITICAL THINKING STRATEGY

Summarizing information

After you read something, it is helpful to **summarize** what you read. When you summarize, you restate the main ideas in your own words. Summarizing will help you identify and understand the most important information.

Follow these steps to summarize a text.

1. Number the paragraphs in the text. Then ask yourself for each paragraph, what is the most important information? For example, look at paragraph 1 in Reading 1.

2. Write the paragraph numbers and your notes on a separate piece of paper. Here are the notes for paragraph 1:

   Paragraph 1 note: blind person—problems in daily life

3. Review your notes. Do they include the main ideas of the reading?

4. Write a summary. Use your notes to write sentences. Here is a summary sentence for paragraph 1:

   A blind person has many problems in daily life.

Notice that the summary is a new sentence, not a sentence from the paragraph.

iQ PRACTICE Go online to watch the Critical Thinking Video and check your comprehension. *Practice > Unit 8 > Activity 4*

D. RESTATE Work with a partner. For each paragraph in Reading 1, write notes to summarize it.

Paragraph 1: _blind person—problems in daily life_____

Paragraph 2: _____

Paragraph 3: _____

Paragraph 4: _____

Paragraph 5: _____

E. RESTATE Use your notes from Activity D to write a summary of Reading 1.

_A blind person has many problems in daily life._____

_____

_____

_____

_____

_____

WRITE WHAT YOU THINK

A. EXTEND Work with a partner. Reading 1 gives one example of a daily activity that is difficult for a blind person (cooking). What other activities are hard for a blind person? List five activities. Circle the one that you think is the most difficult.

_____ _____ _____

_____ _____

A blind man learns to surf with the help of a volunteer for See Surf, a group that helps blind people.

B. DISCUSS Discuss these ideas in a group. Think about the Unit Question, "How can technology help people?"

1. Choose one of the activities you listed in Activity A. Explain how using the Be My Eyes app can help a blind person.

2. The Be My Eyes app is also good for volunteers. A volunteer can quickly and easily help a blind person. It doesn't take much time to volunteer, but you can help someone. Would you like to be a Be My Eyes volunteer? Why or why not?

C. SYNTHESIZE Choose and write the number of one of the ideas from Activity B. Then write a response. Look back at your Quick Write on page 143. Think about what you learned.

Idea: ____

My response: _____

_____

_____

_____

An Extraordinary Scientist

You are going to read an article from a news magazine. The article is about a scientist. Use the article to find information and ideas for your Unit Assignment.

PREVIEW THE READING

A. VOCABULARY Here are some words from Reading 2. Read the sentences. Then write each underlined word next to the correct definition.

1. My father's business is very <u>successful</u>. He has many customers.

2. I hope that I <u>pass</u> this important math test.

3. Did you <u>decide</u> on your vacation? Where are you going?

4. My aunt had a long <u>career</u> in education. She was a teacher for 35 years.

5. The <u>invention</u> of the telephone was a very important event in history.

6. When I was young, my <u>dream</u> was to be an astronaut.

7. I <u>believe</u> that good schools are important for children.

8. I'm not very good at math. My new math class will be a <u>challenge</u>.

VOCABULARY SKILL REVIEW

In Unit 7, you learned to use word families to expand your vocabulary. What is the noun form of the vocabulary word *believe*? Use your dictionary.

a. _____ *(noun)* something nice that you hope for

b. _____ *(noun)* a new or difficult thing that makes you try hard

c. _____ *(noun)* a job you learn to do and then do for many years

d. _____ *(adjective)* doing something well

e. _____ *(verb)* to do well enough on an exam or test

f. _____ *(verb)* to choose something after thinking about the possibilities

g. _____ *(verb)* to think that something is true

h. _____ *(noun)* something made for the first time

iQ PRACTICE Go online for more practice with the vocabulary.
Practice ＞ Unit 8 ＞ Activities 6–7

Scientists in a laboratory

B. PREVIEW Before you read about a scientist, think about words related to the topic. Which words do you think are in the article? Underline them.

businesses	dream	experiment	laboratory	professors
challenging	exams	hospital	medical	scientist

C. QUICK WRITE Write a few sentences about a scientist or teacher you know. How does the person help people? Does the person have a good job? Why or why not? Use this section for your Unit Assignment.

_____

_____

WORK WITH THE READING

A. INVESTIGATE Read the article. Find information about how one person worked very hard to reach her goal.

AN EXTRAORDINARY SCIENTIST

1   Young Saudi Arabian student Hayat Sindi had a **dream**. She wanted to become a great inventor. She wanted to improve health care for all. Her **challenge** was to get the right education. When she was a high school student, she **decided** that she needed to study in England. At first, her parents said no. But Sindi was an excellent student. Finally, her parents agreed.

2   When Sindi arrived in England at age 16, she spoke very little English. Her first year in England was not easy. She studied English and watched hours of television every day. Slowly, her English improved.

3   Her next big challenge was to enter a university program. For 12 months, she studied for the university entrance exams—all in English. After that year, she took the exams and **passed**. Sindi became a student at King's College London. She graduated with a bachelor of science[1] degree. After that, she studied at the University of Cambridge. It was a difficult challenge. Some professors didn't

---

[1] **bachelor of science:** a four-year university degree in science

believe a Saudi Arabian woman could succeed. But she continued to work hard. She was the first Saudi woman to receive a PhD in biotechnology from the University of Cambridge.

4   Today, Sindi is a famous Saudi Arabian scientist. She has a very **successful career**. Just as important, Sindi is a role model[2] for young people in Saudi Arabia.

5   Her dream was to bring health care to all. She is making her dream come true in Africa. In parts of Africa, many people live far from cities and towns. They cannot get simple laboratory tests. So Sindi's organization, Diagnostics for All, made a simple, cheap way to do lab tests.

6   The **invention** is a very small piece of paper with special chemicals. When a nurse puts a drop of blood on the paper, the chemicals change colors. The nurse can quickly look at the colors and read the results. Before this invention, patients waited weeks for results. Often, patients never had a lab test. Now, this simple test helps save many lives.

7   Sindi thinks it's important to have a dream. She also believes that challenges are important because they are part of life's journey[3]. She says, "And most of all, since it's a journey into the unknown, try to enjoy the ups and downs of the ride!"

[2] **role model:** a person you like and try to copy
[3] **life's journey:** the trip of life, from childhood through adult life

B. IDENTIFY Put the events in the correct order. Number them 1–6.

____ a. She graduated from King's College.

____ b. She worked with her organization, Diagnostics for All.

____ c. Hayat Sindi left home to study in England.

____ d. She graduated from the University of Cambridge.

____ e. She passed her university entrance exams.

____ f. She studied hard to improve her English.

Graduates from the University of Cambridge

C. IDENTIFY Complete the statements. Use information from the article.

1. Hayat Sindi was a top student in _____, so she thought studying in England would be easy.

2. She left home when she was _____ years old.

3. At first, her biggest problem in England was her poor _____.

4. She got a bachelor of science degree from _____.

5. Some of her professors at _____ didn't believe she could complete the program.

6. Her dream to become a great _____ came true.

D. EXPLAIN Answer the questions. Write complete sentences.

1. Why did Hayat Sindi want to go to England?

   _____

2. What was Sindi's first challenge in England?

   _____

3. How did she improve her English?

   _____

4. What did scientists at the organization Diagnostics for All invent?

   _____

5. Why do you think Sindi is a good role model for young people?

   _____

E. CATEGORIZE Read the phrases about Hayat Sindi. Write *D* (decision) or *E* (event). A decision is a choice. An event is something that happens.

1. _D_ got permission from her parents to go to England

2. ____ arrived in London

3. ____ passed her university entrance exams

4. ____ received a PhD from the University of Cambridge

5. ____ helped bring health care to more people in Africa

F. EVALUATE For Sindi, what was probably the most important event? What was the most important decision?

   _____

   _____

WORK WITH THE VIDEO

A. PREVIEW In some countries, people do not have electricity. Why is that a problem?

VIDEO VOCABULARY

fuel (n.) anything that you burn to make heat or power

attach (v.) to join or fix one thing to another thing

solar panel (n. phr.) a flat piece of metal and glass that uses the sun to make energy

translator (n.) a person who changes what is said in one language to another language

product (n.) something that people make to sell

iQ RESOURCES Go online to watch the video about one solution for electricity in India. *Resources > Video > Unit 8 > Unit Video*

B. APPLY Watch the video two or three times. Complete the sentences with words from the box.

customers	electricity	light	solution
difficult	kerosene	solar panel	

1. In India, there are many people who don't have good _____.

2. A company called d.light makes lights that are safer and brighter than _____ lamps.

3. The light uses a(n) _____ to get energy from the sun.

4. The first product was _____ for people to use.

5. Two people from d.light went to India to talk with _____ about the problem.

6. After the trip, d.light decided that the _____ was a new product design.

7. The new _____ is easier to use and cheaper to make.

C. DISCUSS Discuss the questions with a group.

1. What are the problems with using kerosene fuel in the home?

2. How would your daily life change if you didn't have electricity in your home?

3. What other recent inventions are improving people's lives?

WRITE WHAT YOU THINK

SYNTHESIZE Think about Reading 1, Reading 2, and the unit video as you discuss these questions. Then choose and write the number of one question. Then write a response.

1. How do the inventions you learned about help people?

2. How does technology help you in your daily life? Choose one example and explain it.

3. What cell phone app do you think helps the most people? Why?

Question: _____

My response: _____

_____

_____

_____

_____

BUILDING VOCABULARY Using the dictionary

Most words have several meanings. When you **use a dictionary**, first find the word and the correct word form (noun, verb, adjective, etc.). Then scan the definitions. Choose the correct definition for the context of the word. (The context is the sentence the word is in.)

☐ Diagnostics for All made a simple, cheap way to do lab tests.

Read the definitions. The correct definition for the context in the sentence above is definition 1.

> **cheap** /tʃip/ *adjective* (**cheap·er**, **cheap·est**)
> **1** costing little money: *That restaurant is very good, and relatively cheap.* ◆ *Computers are getting cheaper all the time.* ➲ **ANTONYM expensive**
> **2** low in price and quality: *I don't like that dress – it looks cheap.*
> **3** not wanting to spend money: *He's too cheap to take her out to a nice restaurant.*

All dictionary entries adapted from the *Oxford American Dictionary for Learners of English* © Oxford University Press 2011

A. IDENTIFY Read the sentences below. Then scan the dictionary entries and definitions. Write the letter of the entry and number of the definition that matches each sentence (*a1, a2,* etc.).

a.
con·tin·ue /kən'tɪnyu/ *verb* (con·tin·ues, con·tin·u·ing, con·tin·ued)
1 to not stop happening or doing something: *If the pain continues, see your doctor.* ◆ *The rain continued all afternoon.*
2 to start again after stopping: *Let's have lunch now and continue the meeting this afternoon.*
3 to go farther in the same direction: *We continued along the path until we came to the river.*

c.
dream¹ /drim/ *noun* [count]
1 pictures or events that happen in your mind when you are asleep: *I had a dream about school last night.*
2 something nice that you hope for: *His dream was to give up his job and live in the country.*

b.
or·gan·i·za·tion Ⓦ /ɔrgənə'zeɪʃn/ *noun*
1 [count] a group of people who work together for a special purpose: *He works for an organization that helps old people.*
2 [noncount] the activity of planning or arranging something; the way that something is planned or arranged: *She's busy with the organization of her daughter's wedding.*

d.
pass¹ /pæs/ *verb* (pass·es, pass·ing, passed)
1 to go by someone or something: *She passed me in the street.* ◆ *Do you pass any stores on your way to the station?*
2 to give something to someone: *Could you pass me the salt, please?*
3 to do well enough on an examination or test: *Did you pass your driving test?* ⊃ **ANTONYM** fail

_____ 1. Sindi's **dream** was to bring health care to all.

_____ 2. Her first challenge in England was to **pass** the entrance exams.

_____ 3. Sindi works with the **organization** Diagnostics for All.

_____ 4. Sindi **continues** to be a role model for young scientists.

TIP FOR SUCCESS
Some words have the same word form for the noun and the verb. For example:
*I had a **dream** about school last night. I often **dream** about school.*

B. APPLY Complete each sentence with one of the words from Activity A. Write the number of the correct definition from that entry.

_2_ 1. The school sports day was terrific. The _____organization_____ of the event was excellent.

_____ 2. Drivers shouldn't _____ other cars when they can't see clearly.

_____ 3. The boy woke up from a bad _____.

_____ 4. After you turn on First Street, _____ straight ahead to the traffic light.

_____ 5. If you want to _____ the test, review your notes.

_____ 6. This _____ helps residents improve their neighborhood.

_____ 7. Let's take a break. We can _____ studying after lunch.

_____ 8. My _____ did not seem possible, but I finally won a school race.

iQ PRACTICE Go online for more practice using the dictionary.
Practice ⟩ Unit 8 ⟩ Activity 8

WRITING

OBJECTIVE ▶ At the end of this unit, you are going to write about how technology can help people. Your sentences will include information from the readings and your own ideas.

GRAMMAR Simple past with regular and irregular verbs

The **simple past** describes completed actions in the past.

- Last summer, he **decided** to attend a community college.
- I **graduated** from high school last year.

Many verbs have **irregular past forms**. (They don't end in -ed.)

Irregular past forms

come	**came**	give	**gave**	leave	**left**	spend	**spent**
do	**did**	go	**went**	make	**made**	take	**took**
get	**got**	have	**had**	see	**saw**	write	**wrote**

- For affirmative statements, use the same past form for all subjects. For negative statements, use *did not* or *didn't* + base verb.

Affirmative statements

subject	verb	
I / You / We / They	**moved**	to this city in 2009.
He / She / It	**came**	to my house last night.

Negative statements

subject	*did + not*	verb	
I / You / We / They	**did not**	**continue**	the game.
He / She / It	**didn't**	**come**	to class yesterday.

- For questions, use *did* + base verb or *wh-* word + *did* + base verb.

Yes/No questions

did	subject	verb	
Did	they	**move**	to Dubai?
Did	she	**come**	to class?

Short answers

yes	*no*
Yes, they **did.**	No, they **didn't.**
Yes, she **did.**	No, she **didn't.**

Information questions

wh- word	*did*	subject	verb
Who	did	you	**see?**
What		the teacher	**say?**

Answers

past verb
I **saw** the teacher.
She **said,** "No."

iQ RESOURCES Go online to watch the Grammar Skill Video.
Resources > Video > Unit 8 > Grammar Skill Video

A. APPLY Complete the sentences. Use the correct form of the irregular verb. Some sentences need the negative form.

1. I ____*didn't meet*____ (not, meet) my friends today. I met them last night.

2. Last night Jomana _____ (give) her friend some advice about college.

3. Jomana _____ (tell) her friend about her college classes.

4. Sarah's family _____ (come) to this country five years ago.

5. My team _____ (win) the final game last year. We were very excited.

6. We _____ (not, leave) at 10:30. We left at noon.

7. Last year, Howazen _____ (have) trouble with her math class.

8. David _____ (not, speak) English when he came here. He spoke Spanish.

9. I _____ (send) you an email last night.

10. Yesterday Sam _____ (take) a driving test. Fortunately, he passed it.

A driving test

B. COMPOSE Complete the questions with *you* and the correct form of the verb. Then answer the questions. Use complete sentences.

1. Where _____ did you go _____ (go) yesterday?

   I went to school, and in the afternoon, I went to soccer practice.

2. _____ (take) a test last week?

   _____

3. Who _____ (speak) with last night?

   _____

4. _____ (have) lunch at school yesterday?

   _____

5. Who _____ (send) an email to yesterday?

   _____

6. How _____ (get) to school today?

   _____

7. How much money _____ (spend) yesterday?

   _____

8. Who _____ (see) last weekend?

   _____

C. IDENTIFY Find and correct the errors with the simple past. Write C next to the sentences that are correct.

____ 1. I have a very funny dream last night.

____ 2. My father graduate from a top university.

____ 3. He no spend very much money during his trip last month.

____ 4. I got a package in the mail yesterday.

____ 5. It take a long time to get home last night.

____ 6. We gave books to the school library.

____ 7. She no did do her homework last night.

____ 8. My friend make a special cake for me last week.

____ 9. They didn't go to the soccer game.

____10. I am seeing my friends in the park yesterday.

iQ PRACTICE Go online for more practice using the simple past with regular and irregular verbs. *Practice > Unit 8 > Activity 9*

iQ PRACTICE Go online for the Grammar Expansion: simple past action verbs and *be*. *Practice > Unit 8 > Activity 10*

WRITING SKILL Writing sentences with *and*

A simple sentence has one main idea. But a simple sentence can have two subjects connected by ***and***. It can also have two verbs connected by ***and***.

subject + subject verb
My friends **and** I play soccer on the weekend.

subject verb   +   verb
Alan studies in the afternoon **and** works at night.

A **compound sentence** has two main ideas. Both parts of the sentence have a subject and a verb. The parts are connected by ***and***. There is a comma before ***and***.

subject verb   subject verb
Susan is a top student, **and** she is an excellent tennis player.

subject verb   subject + subject verb
I went to the coffee shop, **and** my friend and I talked for a long time.

A. IDENTIFY Read the sentences. Label each subject *S* and each verb *V*. Underline *and*. Then write the number of subjects and verbs.

1. My brother <u>and</u> I went to the same university.

   Subjects: _2_ Verbs: _1_

2. Faris made a good decision and got a degree in accounting.

   Subjects: ____ Verbs: ____

3. He started his career in banking three years ago.

   Subjects: ____ Verbs: ____

4. He worked long hours and took some special classes.

   Subjects: ____ Verbs: ____

5. In one class, he and his classmates learned leadership skills.

   Subjects: ____ Verbs: ____

6. Last year, Faris became an assistant manager at his bank.

   Subjects: ____ Verbs: ____

B. IDENTIFY Read the sentences. Underline *and*. Write *SS* (simple sentence) or *CS* (compound sentence).

_____ 1. Hayat Sindi was born in 1967 in Makkah, Saudi Arabia.

_____ 2. She attended King's College.

_____ 3. Sindi wanted to study science, and she wanted to study in England.

_____ 4. While at the university, she studied hard and passed her courses.

_____ 5. In 2001, she received her degree from the University of Cambridge, and she started her career.

_____ 6. Her decision to go to England was important, and it gave her many opportunities.

_____ 7. Today she is a medical inventor, and she is a role model.

C. APPLY Combine each pair of simple sentences into a compound sentence. Include a comma before *and*.

1. She studied at King's College. She got her PhD at Cambridge.

   She studied at King's College, and she got her PhD at Cambridge.

2. Richard joined the organization in 2010. He became a vice president in 2015.

   _____

   _____

3. Last year I studied hard. I became a top science student.

   _____

   _____

4. The brothers have a successful restaurant. Many family members work there.

   _____

   _____

5. I promised my family a delicious dinner. They loved it.

   _____

   _____

6. The scholarship was a great opportunity. I accepted it right away.

   _____

   _____

7. My uncle continued to study at night. He received his diploma last year.

   _____

   _____

D. COMPOSE Use the words and your own ideas to write compound sentences.

1. my brother gave me / I

   <u>My brother gave me a new dictionary, and I use it every day.</u>

2. my friend gave me / I

   _____

3. my parents met / they

   _____

4. I read about / I decided to

   _____

5. I am a strong / I can

   _____

6. I got a letter in the mail / I was

   _____

iQ PRACTICE Go online for more practice with writing sentences with *and*. *Practice > Unit 8 > Activity 11*

UNIT ASSIGNMENT Write about how technology helps people

OBJECTIVE ▶

In this assignment, you are going to write about how technology helps people. Think about the Unit Question, "How can technology help people?" Use the readings and your work in this unit. Look at the Self-Assessment checklist on page 162.

iQ PRACTICE Go online to the Writing Tutor to read a writing model. *Practice > Unit 8 > Activity 12*

A. BRAINSTORM Follow these steps.

1. Think of how technology helps you in your daily life. What mobile apps do you use? What do you use the Internet for? Fill in the chart. Then share your ideas with a partner.

Useful technology	How does it help me?

2. Share your ideas with a partner.

3. Circle the three ideas you want to write about.

B. WRITE Use your brainstorm ideas to write sentences about the three types of technology that help you in your daily life.

iQ RESOURCES Go online to download and complete the outline for your sentences. *Resources > Writing Tools > Unit 8 > Outline*

iQ PRACTICE Go online to the Writing Tutor to write your assignment. *Resources > Practice > Unit 8 > Activity 13*

iQ RESOURCES Go online to download the peer review worksheet. *Resources > Unit 8 > Peer Review Worksheet*

C. REVISE Review your sentences with a partner. Read your partner's sentences. Then use the peer review worksheet. Discuss the review with your partner.

D. EDIT AND REWRITE Complete the Self-Assessment checklist. Make final changes to your sentences. Be prepared to hand in your work or discuss it in class.

SELF-ASSESSMENT	Yes	No
Do you use compound sentences with *and*?	☐	☐
Are your verbs in the simple past correct?	☐	☐
Do you include vocabulary from the unit?	☐	☐
Does every sentence have correct punctuation?	☐	☐

E. REFLECT Discuss these questions with a partner or group.

1. What is something new you learned in this unit?

2. Look back at the Unit Question—How can technology help people? Is your answer different now than when you started the unit? If yes, how is it different?

iQ PRACTICE Go to the online discussion board to discuss the questions.
Practice > Unit 8 > Activity 14

Close-up of a replacement shoulder joint

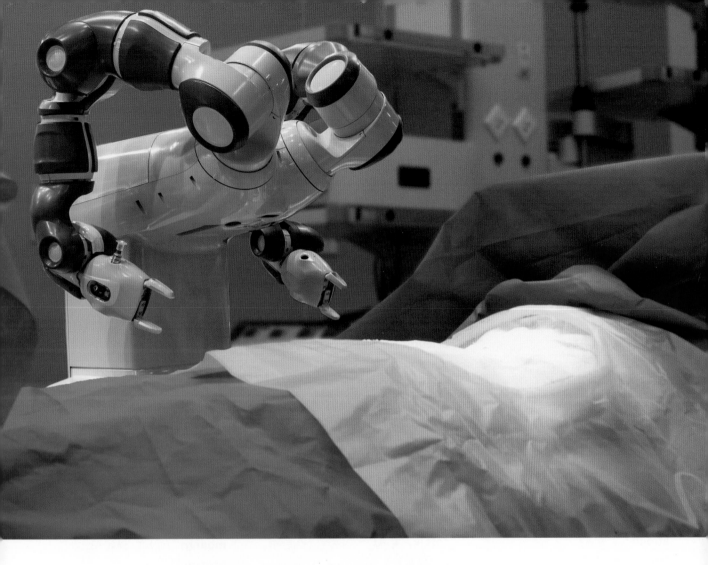

TRACK YOUR SUCCESS

iQ PRACTICE Go online to check the words and phrases you have learned in this unit. *Practice > Unit 8 > Activity 15*

Check (✓) the skills you learned. If you need more work on a skill, refer to the page(s) in parentheses.

READING	☐ I can build reading fluency. (p. 143)
CRITICAL THINKING	☐ I can summarize information from a reading. (p. 146)
VOCABULARY	☐ I can use the dictionary to choose the correct definition of a word. (p. 153)
GRAMMAR	☐ I can use the simple past with regular and irregular verbs. (p. 155)
WRITING	☐ I can write simple and compound sentences with *and*. (p. 158)
OBJECTIVE ▶	☐ I can find information and ideas to write about how technology can help people.

The Oxford 3000™ is a list of the 3,000 core words that every learner of English needs to know. The words have been chosen based on their frequency in the Oxford English Corpus and relevance to learners of English. Every word is aligned to the CEFR, guiding learners on the words they should know at the A1–B2 level.

OPAL The **Oxford Phrasal Academic Lexicon** is an essential guide to the most important words and phrases to know for academic English. The word lists are based on the Oxford Corpus of Academic English and the British Academic Spoken English corpus.

The **Common European Framework of Reference for Language (CEFR)** provides a basic description of what language learners have to do to use language effectively. The system contains 6 reference levels: A1, A2, B1, B2, C1, C2.

UNIT 1
clothes *(n.)* A1
describe *(v.)* OPAL A1
friendly *(adj.)* A1
funny *(adj.)* A1
meet *(v.)* A1
overweight *(adj.)* B2
thin *(adj.)* A2
wear *(v.)* A1

UNIT 2
attend *(v.)* A2
famous *(adj.)* A1
farm *(n.)* A1
feed *(v.)* A2
field *(n.)* A2
flood *(n.)* B1
pick up *(v. phr.)* A2
unusual *(adj.)* A2

UNIT 3
celebrate *(v.)* A2
delicious *(adj.)* A1
event *(n.)* OPAL A1
fresh *(adj.)* A2
grow *(v.)* A1
popular *(adj.)* A1
prepare *(v.)* A1
special *(adj.)* A1

UNIT 4
cost *(v.)* A1
guess *(v.)* A1
idea *(n.)* A1
invite *(v.)* A2
nature *(n.)* OPAL A2
program *(n.)* A2
sightseeing *(n.)* A2
spend *(v.)* A1

UNIT 5
bright *(adj.)* A2
building *(n.)* A1
collect *(v.)* A2
comfortable *(adj.)* A2
contest *(n.)* B2
design *(n.)* OPAL A1
drawer *(n.)* B1
electricity *(n.)* A2
environment *(n.)* OPAL A2
extremely *(adv.)* A2
modern *(adj.)* OPAL A1
own *(adj.)* A1
share *(v.)* OPAL A1
space *(n.)* OPAL A1
spend time *(v. phr.)* A1
view *(n.)* OPAL A2

UNIT 6

be addicted to *(v. phr.)* B2
become *(v.)* A1
behavior *(n.)* A2
break *(v.)* A1
expert *(n.)* OPAL A2
give up *(v. phr.)* A2
goal *(n.)* OPAL A2
instead of *(prep.)* A2
lose weight *(v. phr.)* A2
maybe *(adv.)* A1
pay attention *(v. phr.)* A2
plan *(n.)* A1
stay up *(v. phr.)* B1
stress *(n.)* OPAL A2
unfortunately *(adv.)* A2
turn off *(v. phr.)* A2

UNIT 7

apartment *(n.)* A1
characteristic *(n.)* OPAL B2
complaint *(n.)* B1
crime *(n.)* A2
crowded *(adj.)* A2
homesick *(adj.)* B2
impression *(n.)* B1
improve *(v.)* OPAL A1
in a hurry *(prep. phr.)* B1
international *(adj.)* OPAL A2
market *(n.)* A1
opinion *(n.)* A1
polite *(adj.)* A2
resident *(n.)* OPAL B2
surprised *(adj.)* A2
welcome *(adj.)* A1

UNIT 8

believe *(v.)* A1
career *(n.)* A1
challenge *(n.)* OPAL B1
daily *(adj.)* A2
decide *(v.)* A1
dream *(n.)* A2
explain *(v.)* OPAL A1
independent *(adj.)* OPAL A2
introduce *(v.)* OPAL A1
invention *(n.)* A2
pass *(v.)* A2
quickly *(adv.)* A1
simple *(adj.)* OPAL A2
solution *(n.)* OPAL A2
successful *(adj.)* OPAL A2
volunteer *(n.)* B1

AUTHORS AND CONSULTANTS

AUTHORS

Jennifer Bixby holds an M.A. in TESOL from Boston University. She has taught students of all ages in Colombia, Japan, and the United States in a wide variety of programs, including community colleges and intensive English programs. She has presented at numerous conferences on the topics of materials development and the teaching of reading and writing. She is a coauthor of the *Inside Writing* series published by Oxford University Press. Jennifer is an experienced ELT editor, writer, and author and has worked for many major publishers. Her specialties are materials for adult and university-bound students.

Joe McVeigh holds a B.A. in English and American Literature from Brown University and an M.A. in TESOL from Biola University. He teaches at Saint Michael's College and at Middlebury College and taught previously at universities in California. He has also lived and worked in a variety of countries. He regularly gives workshops and plenaries at ELT conferences around the world. He is a consultant, teacher trainer, workshop presenter, and author; an English Language Specialist for the U.S. Department of State; and serves on the Board of Directors of the TESOL International Association.

SERIES CONSULTANTS

Lawrence J. Zwier holds an M.A. in TESL from the University of Minnesota. He is currently the Associate Director for Curriculum Development at the English Language Center at Michigan State University in East Lansing. He has taught ESL/EFL in the United States, Saudi Arabia, Malaysia, Japan, and Singapore.

Marguerite Ann Snow holds a Ph.D. in Applied Linguistics from UCLA. She teaches in the TESOL M.A. program in the Charter College of Education at California State University, Los Angeles. She was a Fulbright scholar in Hong Kong and Cyprus. In 2006, she received the President's Distinguished Professor award at CSULA. She has trained ESL teachers in the United States and EFL teachers in more than 25 countries. She is the author/editor of numerous publications in the areas of content-based instruction, English for academic purposes, and standards for English teaching and learning. She is a co-editor of *Teaching English as a Second or Foreign Language* (4th ed.).

CRITICAL THINKING CONSULTANT **James Dunn** is a Junior Associate Professor at Tokai University and the Coordinator of the JALT Critical Thinking Special Interest Group. His research interests include Critical Thinking skills' impact on student brain function during English learning, as measured by EEG. His educational goals are to help students understand that they are capable of more than they might think and to expand their cultural competence with critical thinking and higher-order thinking skills.

ASSESSMENT CONSULTANT **Elaine Boyd** has worked in assessment for over 30 years for international testing organizations. She has designed and delivered courses in assessment literacy and is also the author of several EL exam coursebooks for leading publishers. She is an Associate Tutor (M.A. TESOL/Linguistics) at University College, London. Her research interests are classroom assessment, issues in managing feedback, and intercultural competences.

VOCABULARY CONSULTANT **Cheryl Boyd Zimmerman** is Professor Emeritus at California State University, Fullerton. She specialized in second-language vocabulary acquisition, an area in which she is widely published. She taught graduate courses on second-language acquisition, culture, vocabulary, and the fundamentals of TESOL, and has been a frequently invited speaker on topics related to vocabulary teaching and learning. She is the author of *Word Knowledge: A Vocabulary Teacher's Handbook* and Series Director of *Inside Reading*, *Inside Writing*, and *Inside Listening and Speaking* published by Oxford University Press.

ONLINE INTEGRATION **Chantal Hemmi** holds an Ed.D. in TEFL and is a Japan-based teacher trainer and curriculum designer. Since leaving her position as Academic Director of the British Council in Tokyo, she has been teaching at the Center for Language Education and Research at Sophia University on an EAP/CLIL program offered for undergraduates. She delivers lectures and teacher trainings throughout Japan, Indonesia, and Malaysia.

COMMUNICATIVE GRAMMAR CONSULTANT **Nancy Schoenfeld** holds an M.A. in TESOL from Biola University in La Mirada, California, and has been an English language instructor since 2000. She has taught ESL in California and Hawaii, and EFL in Thailand and Kuwait. She has also trained teachers in the United States and Indonesia. Her interests include teaching vocabulary, extensive reading, and student motivation. She is currently an English Language Instructor at Kuwait University.